"'True' is a great place to read about Fabio getting smacked in the face by a bird, French conservative Jean-Marie Le Pen defending male nudity, and a woman who created a ceremony so she could marry herself."

Playboy

"I think that we'd all like to believe that humans aren't as stupid as they seem in Cassingham's column, but we know that sometimes we are. That doesn't make it any less hilarious to read."

Virtual Airlines News Flash

"This stuff is so funny, it can't be real... but it is."

Lockergnome

"Truly valuable."

Salon

"Consistently good humor is hard to find — on the net or anywhere else. Here's a good one."

Internet Tourbus

"Weird News Web Sites: *** (Three stars — Best)"

Infoseek

"This is True finds strange but true news stories, which would be great enough. But ...Randy Cassingham adds the coup de grâce — a witty line that completes each story in precisely the way a news reporter wouldn't dare."

Dummies Daily, "The Web After Five"

What *True*'s Readers Say

"I've almost never received *This is True* without laughing out loud at something within it."

Steve Wozniak, California

"You're providing a great service, making people laugh but also promoting humanistic values of moderation, understanding and plain common sense. Mark Twain would be proud of you!"

Mo, England

"In the 1970s, the *New Yorker* magazine would use — as space fillers — blurbs from newspapers containing typos, grammatical errors, or just plain bad writing. At the end of each was a short comment, witticism or sarcastic statement, but they were always exceedingly funny, written most often by author E.B. White, a man of impeccable grammar, multi-punned witticisms, and a unique and superb writing style. Your intellect and method reminds me of E.B. White's. Your comments are clever, thoroughly insightful, and downright funny. Thanks."

Paul, Minnesota

"Beyond the provision of well written, thought provoking pieces, your ability to use humor to skewer human foibles and blunders is perhaps the single most effective way to provoke change. And failing changes, we then get to share the delights of laughing at others — as we laugh at what is really a reflection of ourselves.

Hal, New York

"This Is True never fails to bring a smile to my face and lifts my spirits by showing me just how silly and absurd people can be."

Eric, Nebraska

"You're absolutely hilarious, articulate and downright funny. What I appreciate most is that your comments/jabs are extremely thought provoking and challenge the commonly held notions. Keep up the great work - I'm sure at least some percent of the smiles & laughs in this world can be directly attributed to you.

Suchit, India

This is True®:
Platform Shoes Claim Another Life
And 500 Other Bizarre-but-*True* Stories
and Headlines from the World's Press

The *This is True* Collection, Volume Six

This is True®:
Platform Shoes Claim Another Life
And 500 Other Bizarre-but-*True* Stories
and Headlines from the World's Press

The *This is True* Collection, Volume Six

---

by

Randy Cassingham

Freelance Communications
Boulder, Colorado

Published by Freelance Communications
Post Office Box 17326
Boulder CO 80308 USA

Printed and bound in the United States of America using non-petroleum ink on acid-free paper.

9 8 7 6 5 4 3 2 1

International Standard Book Number: 0-935309-26-8

Preface . . . .

Welcome to the the sixth *This is True* collection. *True* is a weekly collection of bizarre-but-true news stories with running commentary, plus an actual "headline of the week", that is sold to newspapers and magazines as a feature column. (The first five volumes of the collection, *This is True: Deputy Kills Man With Hammer, This is True: Glow-in-Dark Plants Could Help Farmers, This is True: Pit Bulls Love You, Really, This is True: Artificial Intelligence Like Real Thing* and *This is True: Cost of Being Poor Rising,* are also available — see our web site to order. The titles come from real newspaper headlines.)

I like to make it clear what is it I mean by "true". *True*'s stories don't come from the tabloids or underground newspapers, but rather from the legitimate/mainstream print media, such as national and international news wires, city newspapers, and major newsweeklies like *Newsweek.* But let me caution you: take everything you read in newspapers — and even in *This is True* — with at least a small grain of salt. In addition to my job as a writer, I've worked a few other careers, including a brief stint as a sheriff deputy, several years as a paramedic, and ten years at a NASA field center. One thing in common in all of these jobs is that I have often been a participant in, or direct observer of, events that tend to end up on the news or in the paper. And not once, when I knew the entire story, did any news report on the event come without at least some small error in the "facts".

So I watch carefully for corrections. Whenever I've discovered that an item in *This is True* was based on a "fact" taken in error, or indeed if I've made an error myself, the item has been corrected. But I have resisted the temptation to improve (beyond grammar or typos) my comments — they are as they were written under deadline pressure.

In addition to the print outlets that carry *This is True,* readers can subscribe and get it on the Internet. For details on that, please see http://www.thisistrue.com. You'll be happy to note that even if you've read *True* every week in the newspaper — or online — you still have not read every story in this book. I very often have leftover stories which don't fit in the weekly column (newspapers enforce a word limit). Some weeks have them, some don't, but there are quite a few stories mixed in throughout, plus a section of leftover headlines at the end. Fortunately for me, there is never a shortage of material about the weird things we humans do.

The stories for *This is True* come from "legitimate" printed news media, both American and international. I try as much as possible to credit the original source. For example, if a story is taken from a newspaper, but the newspaper credits a wire service as the source, I do too — I don't necessarily credit the paper I found the story in. Thus the most-cited sources in this book are the major news wires:

- AP (Associated Press)
- Reuters (Reuters Ltd.)
- AFP (Agence France-Presse)
- UPI (United Press International)

This volume compiles columns released to syndication from July 1999 through the end of June 2000.

I enjoy hearing from readers. My e-mail address is included on my web site. After you've had a chance to peruse the stories and headlines here, drop me a line and let me know what you think.

Randy Cassingham
Boulder, Colorado

Edited by Kit Riley
Book and Cover Design by Freelance Communications

"If you can't annoy somebody, there's little point in writing."
Kingsley Amis, British author, satirist

We the People: A survey released for Independence Day in the
U.S. shows that Americans cherish their freedoms. The poll, conducted by Vanderbilt University's First Amendment Center,
found the most important Constitutional right to Americans is the
freedom of speech, followed by the freedom of religion and the
right to bear arms. But when asked to name any of the guarantees
in the Constitution's First Amendment (freedom of religion, freedom of speech, freedom of the press, the right to peaceably
assemble and the right to petition the government for the redress
of grievances), 49 percent could not name even one. Worse, 53
percent said the press has "too much freedom," and 35 percent
thought the government ought to have the power to approve stories that newspapers publish, up from 20 percent just two years
ago. (AP) ... *"Ignorance, forgetfulness, or contempt of the rights
of man are the only causes of public misfortunes and of the corruption of governments." —Declaration of the Rights of Man
(French National Assembly, 1791).*
Cracked Up: Facing racketeering charges, a reputed New England
mafia operative was granted a court order to force the government
to state whether or not it inserted a radio tracking device in his rear
end. "We can confirm that the U.S. Drug Enforcement Administration did not implant a tracking device in defendant Vincent M.
'Gigi Portalla' Marino's buttocks," said a prepared statement by
U.S. Attorney Donald Stern. Apparently amused by the order, the
statement, issued in response to the order Marino requested from
U.S. District Judge Nathaniel Gorton, added, "we cannot speak,
however, for any extraterrestrial beings." (AP) ... *The tabloid version's headline: "Feds Admit Planting Bugs in Space Aliens".*
Popping Wheelies for the Lord: The Sons of God Motorcycle
Club Ministry has won its lawsuit against the Chosen Sons of God
Motorcycle Club Ministries. In their federal trademark infringe-
ment suit in Dayton, Ohio, the party of the first part accused the
party of the second part of misappropriating its "Sons of God

Christ-head logo." Judge Michael Merz ordered the Chosen Sons
not to use the logo, but apparently didn't award the Sons of God
any monetary damages. The plaintiffs' lawyer, Aaron Durden,
said the case wasn't "necessarily" about money, despite asking
for $500,000 in the suit. "Whoever owns that symbol is able to
walk amongst these bikers and preach the gospel," he said. (UPI)
... *"You shall not make for yourself an idol."* —*Deuteronomy 5:8.*

It's Legislated, not Earned: Louisiana schoolchildren are now
required by state law to respect their teachers. Students must
address all school employees as "ma'am" or "sir", or appropri-
ately address them with a courtesy title (Mr., Mrs., Miss or Ms).
"It'll make a difference. It becomes habitual," insists Gov. Mike
Foster. But eighth-grader Asia Ayman of New Orleans begs to
differ: "Kids don't respect their parents at home. What makes
them think they're going to go to school and respect their teachers?" (AP) ...*A comment that shows the appropriate amount of
respect for state politicians.*

Automatic Prison Term: Larry Donnell "Freaky L" Baldwin, 23,
is accused of carjacking. "He told the woman he had a gun," said a
spokeswoman for the Chapel Hill, N.C., police. The driver ran
into a store and called 911 after the thief jumped into the driver's
seat. His getaway was slowed, however, by his apparent inability
to drive a stick shift. He finally got the hang of it by the time police
arrived. He led officers on a chase, but promptly lost control and
crashed. Baldwin has been charged with assault, robbery and
eluding arrest. (Raleigh News & Observer) ...*Cellmates will
surely give him a new nickname: "Shiftless".*

Entranced: "Right now, any person can just hang out a sign that
they are a hypnotherapist and there are no requirements for the
protection of the public," complains Dwight Damon, president of
the National Guild of Hypnotists. So the New Hampshire-based
Guild is lobbying for state laws requiring licensing of hypnotists.
(AP) ...*Do **not** look the lobbyist in the eyes!*

Slick Joey: Former *Exxon Valdez* oil tanker captain Joseph
Hazelwood, who was in command when it dumped 260,000 barrels of oil in Alaska's Prince William Sound, has started the community service aspect of his sentence for "negligent discharge of
oil". Hazelwood will work 1,000 hours at the Beans Cafe, a

kitchen that serves Anchorage's poor and homeless. (Reuters) *...Where he seems to have a knack at mixing salad dressing.*

Crime Wave: Police in San Diego, Calif., arrested Nicholas Anthony Vitalich, 24, after he reportedly hit his girlfriend several times with a 10-pound tuna. "People will use whatever weapon they have available. In this case it was a fish," a police spokesman said. Two weeks later, commercial fisherman Anthony Scott Tucker, 37, was arrested by San Diego Harbor Police after allegedly hitting a customer with a 20-pound tuna. The victim was treated for broken bones and a concussion. Both men could face felony assault charges. (AP, Reuters) *...And if either victim dies, they could face charges of death with a salty weapon.*

Sweet Dreams: Two German tourists went ahead and slept at the Burgundy Motor Inn in Atlantic City, N.J., despite a bad smell in the room. The next day, they switched to another room; when the maid went in to clean, she found the body of a murdered man under the bed. He was identified as a 64-year-old New York man who had previously rented the room. Meanwhile, several days later, New York City subway conductors realized that a man sleeping on a train was in fact dead. The dead man rode around on the train for four to five hours before someone noticed he wasn't breathing. (AP, 2) *...Just like the employees in the station booths.*

Say it with Flowers

Wife Stabs Husband After He Brings Her Bouquets

Reuters headline

Put a Price on This, Your Honor: MasterCard International's ad campaign which gives prices for various items and then describing the experience of buying them as "priceless" — has generated numerous parodies. But the credit card company isn't laughing at an ad in that style on Home Box Office for its comedy series *Arliss.* MasterCard is suing HBO for $15 million, charging the gag ad "knowingly and willfully misappropriates" its copyrights and trademarks. "The ads are clearly a parody and a permissible form of creative advertising," says an HBO spokesman, but

MasterCard says while a joke is one thing, using their idea for a commercial purpose is another. (AP) ...*Swiping a creative concept: $15 million. Watching humorless banking executives sputter indignantly: priceless.*

Keep an Eye on the Competition: English tourist trap London Dungeon has a new gimmick to attract visitors to its "17th century Newgate Jail" exhibit: it's selling fake human eyeballs, hands and feet. "In the 17th century people did buy the remains of executed criminals to use as talismans to ward off evil spirits," a Dungeon spokesman claims. But other tourist attractions find the concept sick. "Everyone enjoys a joke," says a spokesman for the Big Bus Company. But "the majority of our visitors are from abroad and simply aren't prepared for the twisted British sense of humor." (Reuters) ...*If we can stomach Charles in a kilt we can take anything the Brits dish up.*

The Naked and the Damned: Students at Cherry Street Elementary School in Panama City, Fla., were encouraged to bring reading material from home in case they finished a test early. But when teacher Wanda Nelson saw what fourth-grade student Sebastian Allen, 10, was reading, she yanked it out of his hands, declared it "pornography", ripped it up and threw it into the trash. Sebastian was reading a "rare collector's issue" of *National Geographic* which included drawings of naked humans. The teacher was given a written reprimand by the school for "inappropriate action". (AP) ...*And was made to write on the board "I will listen to the defense before passing judgement" 100 times.*

Job Goes Down the Drain: A policeman in Harare, Zimbabwe, was arrested after allegedly accepting a bribe. But the cop ate the evidence, two Z$100 bills (US$5.30), before the arresting officers could grab them. Without the evidence, they don't have a case. "We tried to make him vomit, but it did not work," an investigator said. "So we are waiting for him to release [the money] through other means." (AFP) ...*It's a dirty job, but someone has to do it.*

Next Case: Beverley Lancaster, 44, retired from her clerk job at the City Council in Birmingham, England, because of job stress. What was so stressful? She was promoted against her will, she says. A sympathetic industrial tribunal has awarded her 67,000 pounds (US$105,600) in compensation. "My employers should have listened to me but I was treated like a number, not a human being," she complained. (Reuters) ... *"But 67,000 is a number I can live with," she said afterward.*

Posted: The city of Des Moines, Iowa, is tired of residents putting up signs on utility poles. Signs for garage sales, lost pets, political candidates, weight loss schemes and the like. "It looks really tacky," complains Councilman Michael McPherson. So the city plans to post signs to remind residents that putting signs up on utility poles is illegal. Where will they post these warnings? On the only thing handy: utility poles. (AP) *...Do as we legislate, not as we do.*

Standard Deduction: New Zealand's Parliament asked for documentation from the Inland Revenue Department about what guidelines it uses to determine what is tax-deductible. The IRD responded with 35,000 pages of rules. Among them, the *Evening Post* newspaper found, are rules for prostitutes. Even though the sex trade is illegal, prostitutes must pay taxes. But first, they can deduct their costs for on-the-job bubble bath, dairy whip, condoms, lubricants, lingerie and see-through clothing. "Ordinary stockings are not tax deductible but patterned stockings used for work are," the *Post* found. (Reuters) *...While tax auditors are allowed to deduct whips, pliers, hammers, bamboo shoots and any salt rubbed into wounds.*

Congenital: While medical science can help some men with low sperm counts father children anyway, the children may also suffer fertility problems, researchers say. In some cases, in-vitro fertilization "does result in some men passing the genetic flaw responsible for their infertility on to their sons," says Dr. David C. Page of the Massachusetts Institute of Technology's Whitehead Institute for Biological Research. (AP) *...Leave it to science to turn the perfectly good punchline "If you're infertile it's likely your children will be too" into a recognized medical fact.*

Have You Lost Your Mind? Deborah Lee Benagh, 44, says she was not securely strapped in when riding a roller coaster at Six Flags Elitch Gardens in Denver, Colo., two years ago, and the resulting head-banging caused her to suffer memory problems. "I could have a conversation with someone and turn around and have no memory of it," Benagh said. "I would lose time. I'd be standing at the stove with a spice in my hand and couldn't remember if I'd used it or not." She is suing the amusement park claiming the ride is defective. The roller coaster's name: Mind Eraser. (Denver Rocky Mountain News) ...*How can she be sure that's where it happened?*

Fore!

Golfer Charged With Drunken Driving

AP headline

What a Doll: When you raise the right arm on Mattel's "Rad Repeatin' Tarzan" doll, its "jungle yell" recording plays. But "that right arm is the topic of controversy," Mattel spokeswoman Sara Rosales admits. It seems that pushing the spring-loaded arm down reaches its hand toward Tarzan's loincloth, and repeated action is ...*um*... "suggestive". Rosales adds that "adults look at things through a different set of eyes. Kids have a much more innocent concept." Mattel will not change the doll's design, but will fix the packaging so the "suggestive" arm motions are impossible until the buyer unwraps the doll outside the store. (AP) ...*That's something best done in private anyway.*

Hey, Doll! Push My Button! II: When Tamantha Brannon was shopping at an Atlanta, Ga., Toys 'R' Us store, her 11-year-old son Marvin picked up an "Austin Powers" doll and pushed its talk button. "Do I make you horny, baby? Do I?" the doll demanded. When Marvin asked her what "horny" meant, Brannon was so angry that she has filed a criminal obscenity complaint with county prosecutors. "This is not acceptable," Brannon said. "My son is not old enough to be talking about sex." Clayton County Solicitor Keith Martin is looking into the complaint, but isn't rushing to press any charges. "I don't know who we would even prosecute," he said. (AFP) ...*Start with Ms Brannon.**

500 Channels, Nothing is On: The Annenberg Public Policy Center of the University of Pennsylvania says that one in five TV pro-

---

* See http://www.thisistrue.com/rant-n-rave.html for the rather interesting reaction this tagline caused.

grams aimed at children have "little or no educational value." Even many shows that are labeled educational or "informative", such as *NBA Inside Stuff,* contain minimal educational content, the Annenberg report says. (AP) ... *Whereas four out of five programs targeted toward adults have little or no educational value.*

Civil in his Disobedience: Clifton Courtney Moss, 75, has pleaded guilty after firebombing Australia's Parliament House in Canberra. "I was surprised to get one off. Two was a bonus," he told officers who grabbed him before he could throw a third. The firebombs caused minor damage to the building, and Moss faces up to 15 years in prison on charges of arson and damaging property. Several years ago, Moss had smashed his car into the building's foyer. The gasoline bombs were to protest a bill for A$55,000 (US$36,500) he had received to pay for the damage he caused in the car crash. (Reuters) ... *You can fight city hall, but your choice of weapons is limited.*

Face the Nation: Baltimore, Md., mayoral candidate Dorothy Jennings, 57, appeared on a local news show to talk about her campaign. One of her topics: crime. That caught the attention of an off-duty police officer who was watching the news. He recognized Jennings as Dorothy Joyner, whom he knew to be wanted for burglary. He called the precinct and alerted them to the situation, and TV cameras recorded her being led away from the TV station in handcuffs. (AP) ...*It's not often that politicians and police can work together to reduce crime so quickly.*

Try Passing a Collection Plate: According to a national survey by the Yankelovich Partners for the Lutheran Brotherhood, six out of 10 Americans turn to religion for guidance in financial matters such as investing. They pray, talk to clergymen, or watch religious TV shows for financial advice, the study found. (UPI) ...*There are few places to get financial advice that are worse than from a guy who has made a solemn vow of poverty.*

Countdown: The United Nations Population Fund declares that on October 12, 1999, there will be exactly six billion people on Earth. Or maybe sooner. Or later. "You can't say exactly when," admits PopFund spokeswoman Corrie Shanahan, but in order to get some press hoopla out of the milestone, they decided to choose a specific date. "It's not entirely arbitrary," Shanahan insists. It's based on worldwide census data, some of which is 10 years old, to which they added anticipated births and subtracted anticipated deaths, which should equal six billion sometime soon. (AP) ...*Save a life, ruin a statistic.*

Big Gamble: Eihab Nassar, 23, was recently hired as a "cash runner" at the Hyatt Grand Victoria Casino in Rising Sun, Ind. Police say Nassar picked up $84,000 in cash from the gaming floor and was supposed to deliver it to a cashier, but instead he went down a back stairwell and took off in his car. An Ohio County sheriff's deputy stopped Nassar about a mile from the casino for speeding, but since the deputy didn't know about the theft, he gave Nassar a citation and let him go. He hasn't been seen since. (UPI) ...*Training Note: define "runner" for new employees.*

Prime Cut: Kitten Reynolds says construction workers in Santa Cruz, Calif., harassed her daily as she walked by. So she dressed up in a costume featuring smoked pork chops covering her breasts and marched in front of the offices of Barry Swenson Builders holding signs protesting her sexual harassment. Reynolds, 36, said women "should not be treated like pieces of meat." A company executive apologized to her. (AP) ...*Next week we'll report on her lawsuit against the company for the injuries sustained when their yard dog attacked her chest.*

Face the Music: Marko Milosevic, son of Yugoslav President Slobodan Milosevic, has opened a new nightclub, supposedly named after pop singer Madonna. Even though it was pointed out that Milosevic spelled the name of his nightclub "Madona", Madonna's spokeswoman says the Material Girl may sue anyway. "I hope he has a good lawyer," she added. (AFP) ...*When informed of the possible suit, Milosevic said the singer was a "real bich".*

Monkey See, Monkey Do Dope: Police in Dhaka, Bangladesh, have captured two monkeys that had been trained to sell drugs to street users. "Munni" and "Hamid" had been trained how to collect the right amount of cash, apparently by its color, police say. "We are exploring if there are more such cases," a police spokesman said. The monkeys have been turned over to the Dhaka zoo. (Reuters) ...*It does give new meaning to "having a monkey on your back."*

Derailed

Thomas the Tank Engine
Discovered Driving Taxi
Reuters headline

www.paranoidpsychoticdelusions.com: Actively psychotic people used to complain that they were victims of CIA mind experiments, or that radio waves were controlling their thoughts. Boring old stuff, researchers report. Dr. Glenn Catalano, a psychiatrist at the University of South Florida says you can now add the Internet to the list of bothers. "That's not really surprising," he says. "Things can seem especially threatening when you don't know much about them." One 40-year-old man complained a friend had planted "Internet bugs" in his ears to read his mind, and put special links on his web page that, when clicked on, would cause one of his arms or legs to twitch. Catalano says psychiatrists are "going to have to start asking different kinds of questions" of patients. These days, "you can't just ask if someone is following you." (AP) *...At least web designers now have some great new ideas for extensions to HTML.*

Woo Whee! Max Baer Jr., who played "Jethro" on the 1960s TV series *The Beverly Hillbillies*, is getting closer to building his Reno, Nev., casino based on the series. For instance, says Baer, who's now in his 60s, the "All You Can Et Buffet" will feature extra-large "Jethro hot dogs on Ellie May's buns." The "Shot-gun Wedding Chapel" will feature an optional "Granny" character shooting a scattergun during ceremonies, plus rental bridal gowns with special padding to make the brides appear pregnant. That's not the only planned padding: "We're going to have waitresses dressed like Ellie May but padded like Dolly Parton!" enthused Baer. Tacky? "*Hee Haw* was tacky and was on 14 years. *Beverly Hillbillies* was tacky and was a number-one show," Baer figures. (Reuters) *...Tacky would be a vast improvement.*

Of Their Peers: Helen Schuckman of Fair Lawn, N.J., figures it was the savings account she opened for her daughter that did it: her daughter, Ellie, was put on the county juror's list, and she received a jury summons in the mail. "I mean, she's a bright

3-year-old," Helen says, "but I don't think she's ready to sit on a jury. She might stand in front of the judge and do a little dance or something, but that's about it." (AP) ...*She's qualified: that's approximately the same mental level as the average O.J. Simpson juror.*

Ripcord: A group of parachutists in the United Kingdom doing demonstration jumps to raise money for the National Health Service has had so many injuries, they're actually a drain on the Service. "I would rather pay them not to jump," complained Scottish orthopedic surgeon Chris Lee. The cost of treating the injured jumpers "is far more than any money raised," he says. "An overweight businessman going up for his once-in-a-lifetime jump to raise money for a children's kidney unit is not the same as a fit paratrooper who has gone through rigorous training." The average cost of treating injuries is about 400 pounds (US$625) per jump, he says. The parachutists generally raise about 30 pounds for each jump, after expenses. One woman who broke her leg in nine places on her first jump agrees. "I'll be doing sponsored silences in future," she said. (London Times) ...*With her husband no doubt being the high bidder each time.*

Do You Hear What I Hear? Former child actress Brooke Shields really enjoyed a recent visit to Egypt as part of "the worldwide LISTEN project," a fund-raising program for children in developing countries. "It didn't matter that I didn't speak their language," Shields said. "I was beyond moved by the children themselves. I was amazed at how none of them were willing to be negative about their lives." (AP) ...*Not in English, anyway.*

Mug Shot: While investigating a car theft in London, England, police found the thief's fingerprints in the car. That was useful, but perhaps not as much as another clue: a camera that was left in the car was still there, and the car's owner had the film developed. "I was looking through the pictures when suddenly I saw my car and some bloke in it with a screwdriver in his hand," victim Matthew Holden said. "When I showed the police they recognized him straight away." Bobbies arrested Lee Hosken for the theft. "We are very grateful to this man for making his own arrest so easy," a police spokesman said. (Reuters) ...*Hosken allegedly told the judge he was "badly framed".*

Just Dessert: Restaurant managers in the Netherlands knew the 54-year-old former tour bus driver "Albert B." well. For 20 years, he would order dinner with wine, and when the check arrived would tell the waiter "You have a problem" — and claim to be broke. He made a mistake, though: he liked a restaurant in Leeuwarden so much that he went back. He has been sentenced to three months in jail for theft. (AP) ... *Where he will serve his time washing the jailhouse dishes.*

Dogged Determination: An unnamed British dog breeder has been sentenced to 18 months in jail after admitting to 23 counts of insurance fraud. The 52-year-old woman kept dead puppies in her household freezer, next to her frozen food, and defrosted one when she was ready to make an insurance claim over the "death" of a valuable animal. She received an average of 500 pounds (US$785) for each one. (Reuters) ...*Prosecutors prove popsicle puppies provided phony proof of passings. Apparently, proper precautions prevented pooch pot-roast.*

Tete á Train: The engineers on two freight trains realized there was no way they could stop in time; they were going to collide head-on. The two Union Pacific trains near Palm Springs, Calif., were each traveling between 15 and 20 mph. When they realized collision was imminent, each jumped off the train, sustaining minor injuries. Nine engines derailed. (AP) ...*What happened to "the captain must go down with the ship"?*

Candid Camera: Police rushed to arrest a hang glider pilot who was taking photographs as he flew over the U.S. Ambassador's residence in Herzliya, Israel. Michael Hochstadter, 46, was grabbed when he landed and questioned for hours about what he was doing. Just photographing the "beautiful homes," he insisted. And the Ambassador's house? "I saw a big American flag there, so I understood it was something American," he said, adding he didn't know he was violating any security perimeters. Police confiscated his cameras to review the photographs, and said that if there are only photos of "beautiful homes" on the rolls, the equipment and photos would be returned and the matter dropped. (AP) ...*But if there's just one photo of a beautiful woman sunbathing, it's off to jail for life!*

Above and Beyond the Call: Marcelo Miranda, a police officer in La Plata, Argentina, got the task of talking an 18-year-old woman out of committing suicide. The woman had climbed a water tower and threatened to jump. Miranda solved the dilemma by handcuffing her to himself, then begging her not to jump and leave his children without a father. She agreed to climb down with him. Meanwhile, Orlando, Fla., police officer Rhonda Huckelbery took a sign language class offered by the department, but hadn't practiced the skill in three years when she was called out for a deaf man threatening to jump off a building. She used sign language to talk him out of it. The man "laughed and said he was coming down because my sign language was so bad that I needed more help than he did," Huckelbery said. (Reuters, UPI) *...Luckily he was able to read between the signs.*

Environmentalism Hits the Big Time
U.S. Army To Use "Green" Tungsten Bullets
Reuters headline

Not Furlong: Gamblers wanting to wager on horse races at Lone Star Park in Grand Prairie, Texas, have it easier than ever. The track has opened four service lanes in the parking lot for drive-through betting. "You just drive right up and make your wagers and pay for them and off you go," says a track spokesman. And it's personal, face to face service, he says, "no Jack-in-the-Box speakers or anything." (AP) *...And so convenient, too! When you lose, they just keep your car.*

Just the Facts, Man: Police in Honolulu, Hawaii, responding to an apartment after a "911" call, were greeted by Denny Usui, 28. They asked to see his grandmother, who lived there, but he told them she wasn't home. After insisting they needed to talk to her, he changed his story, officers say. "Oh, I think she's dead," he told the cops. "She's in the shower." Officers found her, dead, "neatly covered" by a blanket. Usui reportedly told them, "I don't want to say anything else until I speak to my attorney because this is a felony and I never committed a murder before." (Honolulu Star-Bulletin) *...If you give up your right to remain silent, any-*

thing you say can and will be used against you as soon as we finish laughing.

Small Town Renaissance: People living near Lily Glen Park in Ashland, Ore., complained to the county after the Society for Creative Anachronism had a members-only event at the park. The private party, for which the group obtained a county permit, featured a "medieval war" staged with period costumes, including armor. Officials ignored the complaints about the battle. "What can you do?" asked County Commissioner Jack Walker. "I'm not going after anybody with a sword and shield." (AP) ...*The pen, especially when wielded by a bureaucrat, is mightier than the sword.*

Scram: Management at the Warrawong Westfield Mall in Wollongong, Australia, is tired of teens hanging around the entrances of stores to chat. To chase them away, it decided to play Bing Crosby's song, "My Heart is Taking Lessons" over and over on outside loudspeakers. It works. "All the people from Warrawong High used to hang here after school," said a teen. "Now you don't see them." In case the tactic wears off, they're ready to implement phase two: pink lighting to make facial acne stand out. (AFP) ...*Phase three: fun house mirrors to make the girls look fat.*

No, Really! Police have captured Arwyn Carr in Flagstaff, Ariz. Carr, 43, faked his death five years ago while awaiting trial in Florida on child molestation charges. "This is one of the most unusual cases I've worked," said Florida state investigator Bill Gootee, who has been working the case. "Most of them just run." Carr faces life in prison over the original charges. Meanwhile, Arthur Gus Bennett, 45, facing a Marine Corps court-martial for raping several children, including his own daughter, faked his death five years ago by killing a homeless man and leaving the body in his home, which he set on fire. He too was recently found alive, in Utah, and was awaiting transfer back to the Marines when he was found hanging in his jail cell, dead from apparent suicide. (AP) ...*If at first you don't succeed, try, try again.*

Don't Toy With Us: President Bill Clinton announced he was "eager as a kid with a new toy" to meet the new Israeli Prime Minister, Ehud Barak. The idiom didn't translate well into Hebrew. An upset Israeli reporter asked him, "What kind of game do you want to play with him?" Clinton quickly explained he doesn't wish to actually play with the prime minister. "I would never do that. If I were taking a trip to Hawaii, I might say I'm as excited as a kid with a new toy. Doesn't mean I think Hawaii's a toy, if you see what I mean." (Reuters) ...*Right. It's not a "Clinton toy" unless she's under 25.*

Absolutely, Positively: Federal Express has lost 695 unscored answer sheets for the Scholastic Assessment Test taken by students in Gardena, Calif. The high school kids that took the multi-hour test will have to retake it, said officials from Educational Testing Service, which administers the college entrance exam. ETS notified the students of the lost tests by mail. "She read the letter, then read the letter again," said one parent, and "she said, 'Mom, there's no score.' Things were coming out of my daughter's mouth I didn't think she knew." (AP) ...*She should ace the verbal portion, then.*

Vroom: Horror writer Stephen King is back to his writing. King, the author of such books as *Cujo, Carrie* and *Misery,* was out walking near his home in Maine recently when he was struck from behind by a minivan, causing serious injuries. King went through five rounds of surgery to repair broken bones and a collapsed lung, but is now home recuperating. He spends "more time out of bed every day, using a walker or wheelchair," his spokeswoman says, and is back "working on a couple of projects he had put on hold." (UPI) ...*Coming soon:* Christine II.

Bring Me Men: U.S. Air Force 1st Lt. Ryan Berry, 26, says he should not have to work with women. Berry is assigned to a nuclear missile silo at North Dakota's Minot Air Force Base. The job requires two officers to be present to launch missiles in case of war. His commanders tried to accommodate his wishes until fellow officers complained about the special treatment Berry was getting. Berry, who is married and describes himself as a devout Roman Catholic, says he cannot work alone with a woman on the typical 24-hour shifts underground because such "close quarters can tempt a man to sin." (AP) ...*If he has no willpower, do we really want him to hold the keys to nukes?*

Spam: The U.S. Congress proudly trumpeted the fact that it e-mailed legislation to President Clinton. The bill, a "Year 2000" legal reform measure, was "signed" using light pens on a computer screen by House Speaker Dennis Hastert and Senate President Pro Tempore Strom Thurmond, witnessed by a gaggle of congressmen huddled around the terminal, and sent by e-mail to Clinton's "President@whitehouse.gov" mailbox. But since electronic signatures are not legal for such documents, a traditional copy on parchment, hand signed, was delivered to the White House later. (AP) ...*Which was a good thing, since the immediate electronic response was "550: User Unknown".*

Out of the Frying Pan, Into the Fire
Scared of Y2K? Head for a Nuclear Reactor
Reuters headline

Personal Foul: Fourteen football players from the University of California at Los Angeles have agreed to plead guilty to illegal possession of handicapped parking permits, which allowed them to park in reserved spaces close to classes and avoid parking fees. They were also charged with giving false information to the state Department of Motor Vehicles in order to obtain the special privileges. The misdemeanor charges could have resulted in 6 months in jail and a $1,000 fine, but the players have agreed to a plea bargain and accept sentences of 200 hours of community service and a $150 fine. (AP) ...*After finally being convinced that mental deficiency did not qualify them for the permits.*

Technical Foul: St. Louis (Mo.) Rams linebacker Leonard Little pleaded guilty last month to involuntary manslaughter charges after running a red light and crashing into a 47-year-old woman, killing her. Police said that Little was legally drunk. The guilty plea gave the National Football League what they needed take action: they have suspended Little from playing in eight games for violating the League's substance abuse policy, though they are allowing him to practice with the team and play in exhibition games. (UPI) ...*That'll teach him.*

Joystick: Billy Mitchell, 34, has become the first person to get a perfect score in the 19-year-old Pac-Man video game. "This was the race to the Holy Grail," Mitchell said after the 3,333,360-point six-hour game in Weirs Beach, N.H. "At about 1.9 million [points], I went off pattern," he said. "I said to myself, 'I didn't come this far to lose.' I started talking out loud to myself, talking my way through it. I was able to cheat death, so to speak." Mitchell also holds the world record for the video game Donkey Kong, which he set when he was 17. (AP) ...*How "hero" is defined in the USA.*

Wanna-be a Hero II: The City of Huntington Beach, Calif., is having a hard time keeping its beach lifeguard towers staffed. During its recent recruitment drive to fill 30 lifeguard openings, only 20 of the 129 candidates were qualified. A half-mile swim to the end of the city pier and back, designed to test endurance, resulted in the rescue of six of the would-be lifesavers. One they didn't even allow to get into the water: on her application, she wrote under swimming experience, "I have none, but I watched *Baywatch* and I look good in a bikini." Lifeguards Capt. Steve Seim said it was typical to get unqualified applicants. "Every year we get people who try out who have no business [being here]." (Reuters) ...*Supervisors nixed Seim's offer to the girl for the position of "training aid".*

All Martha, All the Time: Homemaker doyenne Martha Stewart has filed for a $100 million public stock offering in her company. Stewart, author of 27 books, oversees two magazines, TV and radio shows, an Internet site, a syndicated newspaper column, and a signature line of sheets, garden furniture, paint, kitchen items and fabrics. Her empire raked in $180 million in revenue last year. (UPI) ...*Later, after the stock crashes, we'll show investors how to make some lovely and unique wallpaper.*

Airport Terminal: Florida's Daytona Beach International Airport wants to drum up more business for its little-used runways. One niche they plan to exploit: flying out dead bodies for burial elsewhere. To encourage increased use of their facilities, the airport will give funeral directors 500 frequent flier miles for every body shipped. "We're going after every kind of business we can get," says Volusia County Councilman Big John. "We're going to put this airport back on the map if it kills us." (AP) ...*At which point someone will get 500 frequent flier miles.*

Nyah Nyah: A con man allegedly offered collectable "Beanie Babies" toys for sale on Internet auction sites for up to $1,000 each, and then never delivered after people sent him money. To add insult to injury, he then allegedly posted messages to his victims saying "Ha, ha, ha, ha, ha. Never see the person, never meet the person, never speak with the person and then get upset when you get ripped off. You must be a bunch of morons." That made one victim mad enough that he contacted the Sonoma County, Calif., Sheriff's Department, which has arrested James Denlinger, 28. They say Denlinger may have conned collectors out of as much as $100,000. (Reuters) ... *You've heard that "A fool and his money are soon parted." Now you know how the fool got his money in the first place.*

The Secret to My Success: John McGilbery of East St. Louis, Ill., has turned 100. Asked the secret to his long life, McGilbery said he changed his ways. When younger, "I used to drink whiskey in the morning with my breakfast and play cards with my friends until 4:00 in the morning," he said. When was that? When he was just 85, he said. He's had a lot of experiences, he added. "There's been a lot, and I can't remember most of it." (AP) ... *"Anyone can get old. All you have to do is live long enough." —Groucho Marx (1895–1977), U.S. comic actor.*

Be Seated: Japanese car maker Nissan has introduced the "Nissan bottom". Not a new car line, but an artificial buttocks, clad in jeans, used to test the seats in cars. The bottom simulates getting into the car, settling into position, and getting back out — 15,000 times over a three-day period. "This is equivalent to 32 years of traveling to and from work," a Nissan spokesman said. (Reuters) *...Or an average work day for a mail carrier.*

Base Instincts: BASE ("Building, Antenna, Span, Earth") jumper Frank Gambalie III, 28, liked jumping off stationary objects and popping open his parachute to float to earth. But BASE jumping is illegal in California's Yosemite National Park, so after jumping off El Capitan in the park, rangers moved in to arrest him after he landed. But rather than stop when ordered, Gambalie dropped his gear and dove into the Merced River. His body was found a month later. Shortly after Gambalie's body was recovered, Siddiq Parekh, 31, hiking in Yosemite, stopped to soak his tired feet in the Merced River. He was carried away by the current and swept over Nevada Falls to his death. "The sign essentially says you may die if you swim here, and it says it in several different languages," a Yosemite spokesman said. (AP, 2) ...*Man must respect nature, since nature does not respect man.*

The Royal WeeWee: The faces of Sweden's royal family, including King Carl XVI Gustaf, Queen Silvia, Crown Princess Victoria and Princess Madeleine, have been pasted onto naked bodies and posted on the Internet, the palace has announced, adding legal action was being considered. "We can say without a doubt that this is the worse ever offense against the Swedish royal family," said palace spokesman Elisabeth Tarras-Wahlberg. (AFP) ...*It does, however, beat assassination.*

Someone Forgot
Memorial Pool Now a Crumbled Mess
AP headline

We're From the Government, We're Here to Help You: Sydney, Australia, is sponsoring a legal "shooting gallery" — a safe indoor place for addicts to inject drugs. The facility will be located in the city's Kings Cross nightclub district, and will be run by the Catholic order the Sisters of Charity and St. Vincent's Hospital. "The point about this is to get heroin use off the streets," said New South Wales Premier Bob Carr. (AP) ...*And into church, where it belongs.*

We're From the Government II: A bill before the U.S. Congress would repeal a federal conservation law requiring toilets to use no more than 1.6 gallons of water per flush. The bill's author, Rep. Joe Knollenberg, testified before a House subcommittee that he has received thousands of complaints that "new toilets repeatedly clog, require multiple flushing, and in the end do not save water." Some of the complaints were written on toilet paper, he said. "Their message is clear and straightforward: Get the federal government out of my bathroom." (AP) ...*And into the bedroom, where it belongs.*

Wouldn't Be Able to See it Anyway: A Senate panel in Brazil has approved a proposal to ban the country's flag on women's "dental floss" beach bikinis. "One cannot admit the use of the national flag in situations which are not recommended for the sobriety and the dignity of a symbol of the nation," said a statement from the Senate's Constitution and Justice Commission. (Reuters) *...Indeed. The bikini itself is sufficiently patriotic.*

Straining to Be in the Spotlight: When Vice President Al Gore wanted a photo to show what an environmentally-minded politician he is, he decided a canoe trip on the Connecticut River would do. But to make the photo better, 4 billion gallons of water was released from a dam to bring the river's water level up far enough so Gore's canoe wouldn't get stuck in the mud. "They won't release water for the fish when we ask them to, but somehow they find themselves able to release it for a politician," complained John Kassel, director of the Vermont Department of Natural Resources, to *The Washington Times* newspaper. Kassel later denied making the remark, but the paper stood by its story. Meanwhile, ex-Vice President Dan Quayle is proud that he is the butt of jokes by TV comedians. "In the Leno poll, I'm number one," Quayle proclaimed, referring to the host of *The Tonight Show* who, he says, has made at least 52 jokes this year at his expense. They don't bother him? "Oh, I love those jokes," Quayle insists. (AP, 2) *...At least, the ones he understands.*

Say It, Then Run: "I don't think it's our job as economists or scientists to withhold truth because some people are not going to like it," says University of Chicago (Ill.) economist Steve Levitt. And what "truth" is that? His study concludes that the primary cause of decreasing crime rates in the U.S. is the 1973 legalization of abortion. Abortion reduced the number of "kids who are going to lead really tough lives," Levitt says, contributing to about half of the reduction in crime during the 1990s. The study shows that each 10 percent increase in abortions led later to a 1 percent drop in crime. (UPI) *...Maybe it also explains the lack of intelligent politicians.*

Don't Leave the Playground Without It: Antonia Scalise of Rochester, N.Y., thought it would be amusing to fill out a credit card application in the name of her daughter, Alessandra. She accurately stated that Alessandra was 3 years old, listed her occupation as "preschooler", and wrote she wants a credit card even though "my mommy says no." The application to Charter One Bank was approved and the girl was given a $5,000 credit limit. Antonia complained that even though she put down zero income, the girl got a credit card "with a higher line of credit than me and my husband have." Everyone but the bank has a sense of humor about it: "We've taught her to say, 'Charge it'," Antonia says, but the bank has canceled the account. (AP) ...*Preschooler credit line, $5,000. Beating the bank at its own game, Priceless.*

Don't Bug Me: The Canadian Heritage Department spent C$19,000 (US$12,750) on a poll to determine whether a new national symbol should be added to the traditional Maple Leaf: a national insect. Citizens slapped the idea flat: 84 percent of those polled rejected the entire concept. (Reuters) ...*Leading the world to respect Canuck intelligence just that much more.*

Apocalypse Now: The police superintendent in the town of Picui in Paraiba, Brazil, believed rumors that Earth would be destroyed in a solar eclipse. He ordered the release of the three prisoners in the town's jail "so they could enjoy the little time left before the end of the world." He and the three robbers then got drunk together to lament the event. But once he sobered up, he learned that he had been fired by the province Justice Minister for his actions. (AFP) ...*Rumors of the world's demise have been greatly exaggerated.*

Apocalypse Later: The Interior Ministry of Mexico thought it prudent to reassure the country's citizens about the solar eclipse, even though it wouldn't be visible in the country. "There is absolutely no scientific evidence that eclipses are related to, or associated with, disasters or catastrophes," the Ministry warned in a press release. However, the newspaper *Reforma* didn't find the message particularly reassuring. "Government bulletins rarely are in touch with reality," the paper editorialized, "So if we're not careful the world just might come to an end." (Reuters) ...*Rumors of the cause of the world's demise will rather likely prove correct.*

Of Course! One Follows Him Wherever He Goes

Pavarotti Anticipating Eclipse

AP headline

Hide and Seek: Police in Astoria, Ore., stopped to talk to a driver of a car parked in a crosswalk. He had no license, so the chat was prolonged — enough that a passenger, Roberto Valiente-

Martinez, 28, "got fidgety," police said. Very fidgety: after a bit, the man pleaded with Officer William Barnes to help him remove a package of cocaine that he had hidden in his pants, which was apparently leaking and burning his crotch. Valiente-Martinez was arrested and charged with drug dealing and possession. (AP) *...The good news: numbness set in. The bad news: it may be permanent.*

Hide and Seek II: Irma Acosta-Arya, 39, was in court in Hackensack, N.J., to plead innocent to drug possession charges. A sheriff's deputy did a routine search of the defendant and found 21 bags of heroin and 22 bags of cocaine under her wig and in her underwear. Her bail on the original charge was immediately revoked by the judge. (AP) *...The bad news: there are people so dumb they think they can get away with stuff like this. The worse news: it's definitely permanent.*

Hide and Seek III: Pennsylvania State Trooper Jeffrey Seeley made a "routine traffic stop" of a speeding car. He wasn't even going to give the driver a ticket. But "when I asked the driver to get out of the car so I could explain the warning to him, he was acting very antsy," Seeley said, so he asked a passenger to step out also. That's when Seeley got suspicious. "When I asked him if he had drugs or guns or anything illegal, he fainted. He just rolled right back over the guardrail." The occupants of the car were all arrested when a search revealed 10 kilos of cocaine in the trunk. (AP) *...The bad news: they face 25 years to life. The good news: the car wasn't confiscated because it was a rental.*

Hide and Seek IV: A Mexican national trying to sneak into the U.S. thought a good way to get over the border might be to impersonate an American. He chose his identity poorly. "This guy basically cloned the identity of a wanted fugitive," a Customs Service spokesman at Oakland (Calif.) International Airport said, calling the ploy "kind of a loser thing to do." (Reuters) *...The good news: he won't be charged with the fugitive's crimes. The bad news: forgery and identify theft are more serious charges.*

Hide and Seek V: Myner Santiago Martinez, 22, chose the wrong house to burglarize, police say. Investigators allege Martinez broke into a house, but was confronted by the occupant, off-duty Anaheim, Calif., police officer Luis Gasca. Gasca thought Martinez had a gun, so he shot at the intruder. The suspect ran outside and fell into a cactus plant. After pulling himself out of that, he tried to jump a fence — but slipped and fell on it, impaling his groin on the wrought iron. "It wasn't a good night" for the burglar, an investigator said. Martinez was arrested at a nearby hospital. (AP) ...*The bad news: most burglars aren't convicted. The good news: this guy's already been nicely punished.*

To Sleep, Perchance to Dream of TV Options: Coming soon to a bookstore near you: *Shakespeare for Dummies,* designed to bring the Bard to the masses. Written by Ray Lischner, a computer science teacher at Oregon State University in Corvallis, and John Doyle, a British theater director, the book will feature such chapters as "Why Does Everyone Talk So Funny?" and summaries of each play. In addition, the book features baseball-like "scorecards" so the uninitiated can follow the action. For instance, in *Romeo and Juliet,* "first base on a baseball diamond indicates a suitor who woos a lover. Second base is awarded for meeting a lover in private, third base for getting engaged. Getting married is a home run." (AP) ...*The baseball dating scorecard sure has changed over the centuries.*

All Aboard: An unnamed woman complained to Britain's Thameslink rail company about crowded commuter trains — a problem for her since she is diabetic, has low blood pressure, and is pregnant. Thameslink offered a solution: they told her not to travel at rush hour. The resulting bad publicity caused the railroad company to rethink their advice. "We are sorry that the tone of the letter was a little brusque," a spokesman said. So what are they planning to do for the woman? They hope to add capacity. "We are also considering increasing the size of the signs requesting other passengers to give up their seats to mobility-impaired passengers," he added. (Reuters) ...*It makes one nostalgic for the "good old days" when they'd simply increase the size of the stick the conductor would beat passengers with.*

And They're Not Even Red-Faced: The Crayola company is renaming its "indian red" crayon after people complained it was demeaning to American Indians. Following "flesh", which was renamed "peach" since everyone's "flesh" isn't the same color, indian red, which was named after a reddish-brown pigment commonly found near India, will now be called "chestnut". (AP) ...*After rejecting "PC Red".*

And Now, the News: Does watching the news on TV make you ill? "When the audience feels uneasiness or nervousness while watching news broadcasts," it may be "due to the high and irregular frequency of the newscasters' blink rates," says ophthalmologist Kazuo Tsubota of the Keio University School of Medicine in Tokyo, Japan. He says his studies show the typical newscaster blinks four times as much as an average person, which might convey a sense of nervousness. (Reuters) ...*Then why do people still get sick when they cover their eyes?*

Truth in Advertising

"Boom Box" Explodes, One Dead

Reuters headline

Viral Marketing: Roger Freeman, an Encino, Calif., dentist and lecturer on infectious diseases, wants to start an epidemic. Well, not really: his new company is pushing a line of neckties with magnified pictures of diseases from microscope slides. "The gonorrhea tie is the best looking tie in the whole lot," Freeman says, allowing that "The syphilis tie is gorgeous. The plague tie is pretty, [but] it's sold out." In addition, patterns showing tuberculosis, herpes, staphylococcus, AIDS, chlamydia, ebola, influenza and several other pathogens are available. Don't want to wear your favorite disease around your neck? Matching underwear is also available. (Reuters) ...*Next year, he hopes to debut a new line of condoms.*

Fishy Reasoning: Bobbie Tanaka, manager of the Sumo Sushi restaurant in Irvine, Calif., vows not to bend to police pressure. The restaurant sponsors the "Sumo Lobster Hunt" where patrons pay $2 to use an arcade-style claw to grab a live lobster from a tank. A police animal control officer ordered the practice stopped on the grounds it was "in violation of the code of bad taste." But after consulting her lawyer, Tanaka reinstated the dinner game, wondering aloud why police were bothering her about it. "You would think I was standing there beating 'em with a stick," she said. (AP) ...*Actually, that would probably be legal.*

Inside Job: A gang of four bandits armed with machine guns broke into a prison in Tremembe, Brazil, making away with the wages prisoners had earned in jobs both inside and outside the prison. The haul was a good one: 50,000 reals (US$28,000) in cash. "Money is money," a police investigator said. "There are not too many places to rob." But prison director Carlos Corade was incensed. "Bandits robbing convicts is just appalling," he said. (Reuters) ...*Would you have felt better if they robbed widows and orphans, Sr. Corade?*

Das Boots: Police in Leipzig, Germany, have a problem with a 16-year-old boy. Police say the alleged neo-Nazi is responsible for kicking people with his heavy, steel-toed boots, and then for good measure beating them with chains. The unnamed boy has been banned from wearing his boots — and carrying knives, baseball bats and iron chains — for two years. "We consider this a suitable preventative measure toward firmly combating right-wing extremism," said a Saxony state police spokesman. (AP) ...*Here's a radical idea: let's make assaulting people illegal.*

I See the Light: The U.S. Department of Energy is funding a $5 million pilot project to turn sewage into electricity. "The idea is to use the stuff to produce energy rather than have it detract from our land by putting it into landfills and so on," said Otis Mills, spokesman for the DOE's Federal Energy Technology Center in Pittsburgh, Pa. "Initiatives like these prepare America for the next century. We'll never run out of this stuff, obviously. We produce lots of it." (Reuters) ...*And that's just the government.*

My Father's House: Officials from the Federal National Mortgage Association were almost speechless when Norman and Melissa Cameron told them why they didn't plan to pay their $54,000 mortgage. "When I read it, I was taken aback," said FNMA's lawyer. Read what? The Camerons' response to foreclosure proceedings on their Hartford, Conn., house: they claim God told them they didn't have to pay. "It was our desire to be free from this mortgage debt," the Camerons told the court overseeing the foreclosure. "Therefore we asked God our Heavenly Father in the name of Jesus Christ. He heard us and he freed us from this mortgage bondage." (AP) ... *"Give to Caesar what is Caesar's." —Matthew 22:21.*

Dog Days: When nearly 100 Chinese migrants landed on Canada's Vancouver Island, there was such an uproar about the influx of "illegal immigrants" that the government is considering deporting all of them back to China. All but one, that is: a dog that accompanied the group on their two-month ocean voyage will likely be allowed to stay. "She's a very well-mannered, very nice dog," reported a spokeswoman for the Society for the Prevention of Cruelty to Animals in Victoria, though she adds the dog is "kind of frightened, kind of scared, kind of bewildered." (Reuters) ...*Kind of like the immigrants must be.*

Yo Quiero Chihuahua: Mexico's state of Puebla is worried about the area's growing population of stray dogs, estimated to number 1.1 million. So state Health Secretary Jesus Lorenzo Aarun has set up a program to give out 5,000 packages of food in exchange for dogs, which will then be killed. (AP) ...*No! Don't eat it! Don't you know what Soylent Gray is?!*

The Big Picture: While it may seem like you see a complex scene all at once, so-called "parallel processing", your brain actually uses "serial processing" — your eye skips rapidly from one object to the next, says psychology professor Steven Luck of the University of Iowa in Iowa City. "This may seem counterintuitive because it doesn't feel like we perceive only one object at a time," Luck says. "But although it may seem that when you look at a scene, you are seeing the whole picture, each object in the scene commands your attention in rapid succession." (UPI) ...*Your brain only thinks of one thing at a time, too.*

Welcome to the Real World: The latest target for online ads: university students streaming back to school. At North Carolina's Appalachian State University, for instance, students looking at course catalogs on the school's internal web site will see ads for bookstores, computer companies, and apartment houses. AppState associate professor of political science Andrew Koch complains that the school's policy of letting advertising pay for the campus' information infrastructure "tells volumes about the university, its funding, and the business mindset that has taken over. We're throwing our freshmen to the wolves." (New York Times) ...*The TV Generation: smart enough to get into college, yet too stupid to resist ads?*

Peace at Last

Lutherans OK Pact
With Episcopalians
AP headline

A Politician with Teeth: In 1981, Bosco was elected honorary mayor of Sunol, Calif., easily beating out two human contenders. Bosco, a Rottweiler-Labrador mix, died in 1994, but local Mike Cerny doesn't want the ex-mayor of the unincorporated town to be forgotten. Cerny plans to open a restaurant, Bosco's Bones and Brew, which will feature a memorial beer tap — a $3,500, life-sized model of Bosco. To draw a pint, the barkeep just lifts one of the dog's hind legs. (AP) *...Which is also a fitting tribute to the typical American brew.*

Our Next Guest: After several incidents involving "fake" guests on TV talk shows, the Edinburgh (Scotland) International TV Festival hosted a panel discussion of television executives to talk about the problem. "Fake" guests are most often actors paid to promote a cause or pranksters who just want to be on TV. Either way, several scandals have resulted, causing at least one show to be taken off the air. The TV Festival's "Liar, Liar, Pants on Fire" debate was billed as a "lively, provocative and sometimes raucous look at one of the most talked about issues of the television year — chat show fakery." During the debate, it was revealed that one of the panelists — the "researcher for talk show host Jerry Springer" — was a fake. (Reuters) *...Hard: keeping up with the competition. Easier: dragging them down to your level.*

Who Can I Say is Calling? U.S. Justice Department Inspector General Michael Bromwich says that federal prisoners are using prison telephones to commit crimes, and the problem continues despite the fact that the Bureau of Prisons has known about it for over 20 years. "We found various cases in which inmates retained full telephone privileges even after they were convicted of a crime involving the use of prison telephones," Bromwich said. In one case, a drug dealer used a prison phone to order the murders of two grand jury witnesses against him. One was killed and the other was shot, but lived. Even after being convicted for that crime, he still had full telephone privileges and his calls were not monitored, Bromwich said. (AP) ... *Yet your complaint calls to the phone company are "monitored for quality assurance."*

Hard Time II: David Williams, 40, serving a life term for murder in West Virginia's Mount Olive prison, pulled out a gun during a meeting with prison officials and started shooting. He was subdued and no one was hurt. His girlfriend, Anna Marie Thomas, 29, admits she smuggled the gun into the prison in her panties, saying jailers believed her when she told them it was metal in her boots that set off a metal detector. Williams says he had Thomas bring him the gun so he could show it to the warden and tell how he got it in trade for more lenient treatment. Thomas has been arrested, and complains that officials won't let her visit Williams anymore. "I can't write, we can't call, we can't do anything," she said. "It's not right." (Charleston Gazette) ...*They're made for each other: both really put the "I" into "Idiot".*

Hard Time III: Police investigating a burglary in Marion, Ky., saw Justin Jones, 29, in the area. They thought Jones was in jail, so they went to check. Deputy jailer Francisco Barela, 22, said Jones was in his cell, but officers demanded to see for themselves. Jones indeed was not there, but a search of cells found prisoners had cold beer and loaded guns — and one was in bed with a woman. Inmates told police the "party atmosphere" started when Barela started working at the jail. He has been arrested — and is being held in a different jail. (AP) ...*If you can't beat 'em, join 'em.*

So Easy, a Rat Could Do It: Lord Bath's Longleat Estate in Wiltshire, England, holds the record for the longest garden maze. The maze, made from 3.25 miles (5.2 km) of hedges, attracts visitors from all over the world — who promptly get lost. But recently, people in the maze have been calling Longleat's business office on their portable phones for help getting out. "I don't know what they think we can do as we don't know where they are either," says attractions manager Tim Bentley. "Really, if you are going to go into a maze, then you'll get lost. That's the point, isn't it?" (Reuters) ...*Sounds like intentional infliction of emotional distress. Surely a lawsuit will follow soon.*

Strict: Hendersonville (Tenn.) High School Principal Paul Decker is embarrassed over the student handbook, given to new students as they started the new school year. "Profane language will not be tolerated," it says. "Stern discipline will be death to any student guilty of this conduct." Decker says he thinks people will understand "dealt" was misspelled. "Most folks know that it was a misprint," he assured reporters. (AP) ... *"The best lie is the truth told unconvincingly." —American proverb.*

Free at Last? When fifth-grade teacher Barb Vogel told her students at Highline Community School in Aurora, Colo., that children were being sold as slaves in the Sudan, they wanted to do something about it. They raised money to buy more than 1,000 slaves and set them free, and then started to raise additional money to buy more. "Please reconsider," begs Stephen Lewis of the United Nations Children's Fund. "If you can pay for more slaves, undoubtedly more slaves will be provided for you." Manase Lomole Waya, director of Humanitarian Assistance for South Sudan, agrees, saying the buyback program "is not eradicating slavery, it is enhancing it." Publicity over Highline's efforts have spurred similar programs in about 100 other schools, leading to dropping prices for slaves — showing an excess supply and increasing competition among slave traders, anti-slavery experts say. Vogel says she'll let the kids decide whether to continue, but they don't seem to understand the concept of supply and demand — so far, they want to continue the project. (Denver Post) ...*Is this really what people meant when they said schools ought to go back to the basics of the good old days?*

Hot Hot Hot: The Cambridge, Mass., police commissioner has apologized for a training course in the police academy there. Cadets were told that pepper spray was less effective on Mexicans and others who tend to consume spicy foods. "The people that it doesn't affect are people who have consumed cayenne peppers from the time they are small children, and this generally breaks into ethnic categories," claimed a training officer. Pepper spray contains "O.C.", the oily resin of capsicum, the same ingredient in hot peppers. "So, with Cajuns, Mexican-Americans, Pakistani, Indian .... what happens is the O.C. is effective for a much shorter time," the training officer added. "There is no empirical or scientific evidence to support these statements," Police Commissioner Ronnie Watson told papers after the training procedure was made public. (AP) ...*Still, the Mexican officers say it makes a nice enchilada sauce.*

Dead Men Tell No Tales ...Nor Sue

General Motors: Air Bag Failure Not a Concern

AP headline

Why They Call it a "Trap Door": Police in Utrecht, the Netherlands, responding to a burglar alarm at a school found nothing, but employees carefully locked all the doors in the building. Sure enough, a man was hiding in a crawl space under the floor — and found himself locked in. For two days. A security guard finally found him, and provided a long drink of water before letting him go home. Meanwhile, the manager of Ruby's Pizzeria in Deerfield Beach, Fla., found a man in the grill vent, where he had been stuck for 20 hours. A rescue crew had to pour grease on him to slide him out. The unidentified man told police he was just looking for a place to sleep. (AP, Reuters) ...*Nearly for eternity.*

Catch Me If You Can: A wild monkey ran amuck in the "posh" Azabu district in Tokyo, Japan, for months, eluding authorities who tried to catch it. News coverage showed police trying to throw a net over it, and warned people that the monkey could bite. But the macaque met its match when it invaded the American Club. A pool attendant saw it and lured it into an office, locked it in, and called the zoo for help, bringing the months-long ordeal to an end in just a few minutes. (AP) ...*No surprise: when it comes to monkey business, Americans are experts.*

Mr. Missed Mrs.: Nicklaas Amsterdam of Johannesburg, South Africa, recently celebrated his 112th birthday. Asked for the secret of his longevity, Amsterdam said it was all a matter of refusing to have sex. Ever. "I have never had a woman to give me a headache," he said. (Reuters) ...*But without sex, what's the point of living in the first place?*

Rear View Mirror: Andrew Ebner, a volunteer firefighter heading home in his pickup truck after a nighttime fire call in Hagerstown, Md., saw a truck on his tail. That driver started shooting at him with a shotgun, puncturing his tailgate and blowing out his rear window. He knew he couldn't outrun the truck, so he decided to stop and run on foot. Once he got out, the shooter was able to see him — and apologized, saying he was shooting at the wrong guy. Ebner says Kenneth Ramsburg even gave him his business card and offered to pay for the damage. Ramsburg then drove off and, police say, then found who he was looking for and shot that man in the leg. Apparently satisfied, he headed home, passing Ebner again — and two sheriff's deputies taking his statement. The deputies chased him down and arrested him. Ramsburg is being held without bail for attempted murder and driving while intoxicated. (AP) ...*As if I can add anything to that.*

Please Unfasten Your Seatbelts: A new study says once plane crash survivors get over their initial psychological distress, they end up in excellent mental health. In fact, "crash survivors actually scored lower on several standardized measures of emotional distress than the flyers who hadn't been in an accident," says Gary Capobianco of Old Dominion University in Virginia. Going with the flow when an aircraft you're on cartwheels through a corn field helps, Capobianco says. "How the survivors perceived their level of control during the crash seemed to affect their future feelings of distress," he said. "Flight crew survivors who believed they had control over events that may have led to or caused the crash reported less distress." And, he says, some survivors were so mentally healthy that "Future research should focus on how experiencing a traumatic event can actually provide a positive benefit to or become a resource for a survivor." (UPI) ...*Disneyland is right on it. Coming soon, "Carnage Mountain".*

Reinventing Propaganda: The "Reinventing Government" project, spearheaded by Vice President Al Gore, has not saved as much money as Gore claims, according to an audit by the General Accounting Office. The GAO says that $21.8 billion of a claimed $107 billion in savings logged over the last six years cannot be accounted for, in part because savings were counted twice, or the project took credit for cost savings from events they had nothing to do with, such as the end of the Cold War. A White House spokeswoman dismissed the GAO's report, calling it "an arcane debate about accounting." (AP) ...*Al says he was able to end the Cold War in his free time after inventing the Internet.*

This Will Be Funnier If You Read it After Midnight: A hot topic in nutrition research these days is figuring out why some people can't seem to lose weight. Psychologist Timothy Osberg of Niagara University in New York has part of the answer: some people have "irrational beliefs" about nutrition, he finds. For instance, his surveys find that some people actually believe that foods like ice cream have no calories when eaten standing up, that not eating desserts can be dangerous to health, or that anything eaten with your eyes shut "doesn't count". Osberg says his studies show the more such strange beliefs people hold, the more likely that they are obese or have failed to lose weight on diets they have tried. (UPI) *...The question isn't so much are they fooling themselves as are they fooling the researchers?*

Charge It: As students head back to college this fall, they're being greeted by ...credit card applications. Banks view students as a good risk since if they get over-extended, parents will step in. Plus, studies have found, getting consumers into the fold while they're young leads them to become loyal, long-time cardholders. "You give a college kid a credit card and 15 years later they still have that credit card," said an industry expert. (AP) *...And the debt they ran up on it.*

Stereotype Squad: When the holdup alarm came in, police officers in Panama City, Fla., knew right were to go. Two squad cars raced toward the scene — and crashed into each other. The officers were treated for minor injuries and the holdup man escaped. The scene of the crime? The local donut shop. (UPI) *...On the other hand, they weren't already there.*

Sometime, When They Get Around to It

Scottish Scientists Plan Search For Laziness Gene
Reuters headline

To Protect and Serve: Robert Jordan sued the New Haven, Conn., police department after it rejected him as a police officer because he scored too high on an intelligence test [*This is True: Pit Bulls Love You, Really,* p138]. But U.S. District Judge Peter C. Dorsey has dismissed Jordan's suit, ruling that he "may have been disqualified unwisely, but he was not denied equal protection" as defined by law. Jordan's IQ is approximately 125, versus a national average police officer IQ of 104. New Haven argued that a too-smart cop "could soon get bored with police work and quit after undergoing costly academy training." (AP) ...*More likely, the brass realized he'd outrank them within two years.*

To Protect and Serve II: Darryl Ellis, 23, of Gulfport, Miss., was stopped by police for urinating in public. Officers searched him — and found the holdup note from a recent bank robbery in his pocket. The FBI was called in, and Ellis has now been charged with bank robbery. "We're fortunate that some of these crooks aren't too intelligent," a Gulfport police spokesman said. (Reuters) ...*The intelligent crooks are all heading for Connecticut.*

To Remove from Service: When Eric Coley got in a dispute with his employer, they fired him. Coley, the doorman at the Jefferson Hotel in Richmond, Va., says the hotel demanded everything that it owned, including his uniform. "They wanted everything, so I gave them everything — timecard, keys, pants," he said. Then, "I felt I just had to get out of there. If I had to leave butterball naked I would have." Coley then walked out the door in his underwear and down Main Street to his car. (AP) ...*Dignity: walking out with his head held high. Indignity: having to open the front door himself.*

To Heat and Serve: Hamburger giant McDonald's has changed America, sociologists say. The chain's 25,000 restaurants pride themselves on the consistency of their food no matter where it is served, but that has made it "harder to tell where the Midwest ends and the South begins," they say, and the sheer number of McDonald's stores has forced traditional diners out of business. "These small restaurants cannot survive" in the face of competition from McDonald's, says Chicago's Northwestern University sociology professor Gary Fine. Though, he says, "to be honest, those little restaurants didn't serve very good food. We romanticize them but that's the truth." (UPI) ...*So really, then, nothing has changed at all.*

What Happened to Writing a Letter to Your Congressman? Ara Tripp, 38, of Olympia, Wash., climbed a 180-foot high-voltage transmission tower next to a freeway, took off her shirt and began dancing topless for the traffic. Occasionally, she'd take a swig of vodka, then spray it out of her mouth and light it afire. In order to keep Tripp from electrocuting herself, Seattle City Light cut off power to the tower, blacking out 5,000 homes and businesses. Meanwhile, traffic came to a standstill. Tripp said the stunt was to protest "discrimination against women" because laws allow men to take off their shirts in public, but not women. Tripp later said her wife — Tripp was a man, before a sex-change operation — would be upset. "She's not going to be happy. I'm going to be grounded." (AP) *...Topless transsexual Tripp struts atop tower, tying traffic, to attract citizen attention to authoritarian statute, instead triggers trouble with sweetheart.*

What the F- - -? The "F-word" has lost its power. So ruled the Dubbo Local Court in New South Wales, Australia. "F- - -", as the *Sydney Morning Herald* spells it, "has lost much of its punch," ruled magistrate David Heilpern in dismissing "offensive language" charges against a man who told police to *...well... f- - - off"*. Heilpern said he's heard the word several times recently in PG-rated movies, and "We live in an era where Federal ministers use the word over the telephone to constituents and are not charged." He ruled the word's utterance could not be the basis for criminal charges as it "is extremely commonplace now" in public. (Sydney Morning Herald) *...But not commonplace enough for newspapers to print it.*

Recycle This: Gerald Turner, 49, is suing Madison, Wis., garbage hauler Waste Management for discrimination because it turned him down for work as a recyclable sorter merely because he raped and murdered a 9-year-old girl. Turner, also known as the "Halloween Killer", killed Lisa Ann French in 1973, was released from prison in 1992, and is still on parole. Waste Management officials rejected Turner for the job because the plant regularly hosts student and scouting group tours, but an investigator with the Department of Workforce Development noted that "If he were considered unsuitable for the position of sorting recyclables, it would then appear that he could be lawfully excluded from every other job dealing with other people and with most if not all objects." (AP) *...Sounds reasonable.*

Whatever: U.N. Special Envoy Olara Otunu recently visited Sierra Leone and was shocked by the atrocities committed against people in the civil war there. "The magnitude of suffering that I have seen... is beyond belief," he said. He said Murray Town camp in Freetown was "a whole community of amputees — a community of people without limbs." What to do about this tragedy? Otunu says he agrees with the local people. "The children in particular want to see the process of disarmament begin." (Reuters) ... *You know, sometimes it's a poor choice of words that starts wars in the first place.*

Choose Any Five

Compromise on
Ten Commandments
AP headline

Homeless, Sweet Homeless: Marian Neal, 40, was living with a friend in Alexandria, Va., and felt sorry for a 7-year-old neighbor who needed a kidney transplant. Neal was a perfect match, and donated one of hers. Neal, who is on disability for a back injury, was then evicted from her friend's public housing project because roommates are against Housing and Urban Development rules. After a newspaper reporter tracked Neal to a homeless shelter, embarrassed HUD Secretary Andrew Cuomo personally intervened and found Neal her own public apartment. (AP) ... *See? The U.S. is willing to take care of its homeless, but it can cost them an arm and a leg.*

It's a Small, Small, World: Disney Online wants kids to know they need to be safe on the Internet. Its British, French and German web sites recently unveiled a special version of "The Three Little Pigs" to help warn kids of the dangers of "wolves in sheep's clothing", followed by an animated Mickey Mouse warning kids never to give out their address or phone number. They should have posted it in the U.S., too: several days later an executive vice president from Infoseek, a Disney Online subsidiary, was charged with interstate travel with the intention of having sex with a minor. Patrick Naughton, 34, of Washington was arrested after meeting a "13-year-old girl" — actually an undercover FBI agent — in California after several alleged online chats with her. (Reuters, 2) ...*Hi ho, hi ho, it's off to jail you go....*

Luxury Accommodations: Three Old Order Amish men, and one woman, were sentenced to 90 days in the Buchanan County, Iowa, jail after vandalizing an Amish neighbor's farm. But jailers released them after 72 days. "I thought we better get them out of here because they were getting too used to it," said jail administrator Russell West. "I think we were ruining them here. The TV, the electric light, telephone and running water — I think they were starting to like it here." (AP) ...*It's just no fun to punish people who smile in return.*

Poke The Man: Two 9-year-old boys from Long Island, N.Y., say they drained their piggy banks to buy pack after pack of "low-value" Pokémon game cards hoping to find more valuable "rare" cards which are randomly distributed in the packs. This scheme to induce kids to buy the cards is an "illegal gambling enterprise," they say. "You pay to play," says one of the kids' attorneys, "there is the element of chance, and you've got a prize" — the "three elements of gambling," he asserts. Nintendo, which makes the cards, calls the charges "baseless," but the kids have filed a federal racketeering lawsuit against the company. (New York Post) ...*Which is, of course, a form of gambling in itself.*

Truth in Nomenclature: Swedish Integration Minister Ulrica Messing wants to do away with the term "immigrant" in the country's laws and speech. "The label 'immigrant' is connected with a lot of different negative aspects, like unemployment and social exclusion," explains a spokeswoman. "We tend to create a 'we' versus 'them' situation and want to break this up." And what would the new label be? Messing suggests "person of foreign background" would be more appropriate. (Reuters) ...*"Idiot" is too negative. "Person of political background" would be more appropriate.*

Person of Criminal Background II: Police in Hermiston, Ore., checking the area around a bank shortly after it was robbed, heard a man pleading for help from inside a car trunk. An officer opened the trunk and freed Lucas Winters, but not for long: Winters was arrested and charged with the robbery. "We think he wanted to do a quick change, get out of the trunk and walk off in a new disguise," a police spokesman said. "But he got accidentally locked inside." (AP) ...*For 12–20 years.*

Persons of Clueless Backgrounds III: Santa Clara County, Calif., Superior Court Judge Jack Komar's house was firebombed. A 17-year-old boy called 911 to blame the attack on someone else, but police quickly implicated him and two friends, aged 17 and 19, in the crime. But that's not all. "It's very, very clear that the hateful motive involved in this firebombing was because the suspects believed that the [judge was] Jewish," a police spokesman said. The three, who live nearby, are now also suspected in an earlier anti-Semitic attack at the judge's house last year, and have been charged with committing a hate crime, terrorism and arson. Bad enough, except Judge Komar is not Jewish. He's Catholic. (AP) ...*So much for the teens' "supremacy" theory.*

Help Keep a Woof Over His Head: Karen Kuhlman of Ft. Mitchell, Ky., says she doesn't know how her dog, Duke, got on various marketing lists, but the 5-year-old pug has been getting an awful lot of mail. She says Duke has been offered a door-to-door sales job paying "as much as $9 an hour and college tuition reimbursement." Plus, "He gets [credit card offers] as often as you and I get them. He's pre-approved and has a credit limit of $2,000. I tear 'em up. I don't want him running amok with these things." And, she says, he's been reminded to register for the draft, and an art institute wrote, "Duke, our students are a lot like you — friendly, creative, talented and serious about success." (UPI) ...*The sad part is, that's probably true.*

Take 69: With film productions moving to Canada and other cheaper places to work, Hollywood movie-makers are feeling the pinch. However, there is still one segment of the industry that's thriving: pornography. While the industry is down 13 percent, the adult movie industry is up 25 percent this year, with 10,000 porn titles scheduled for release by year-end, according to trade magazine *Adult Video News.* The Los Angeles County Economic Development Corporation says adult films are an increasingly important part of the area economy. EDC chief economist Jack Kyser says that while "you might not approve of the product ...the success of the adult segment is a welcome anchor in the wind." (UPI) ...*Or, it's OK to have standards, as long as it doesn't get in the way of making money.*

Years of Studies Finally Explain

Higher Costs Explain Why
U.S. is Cheaper than U.K.

Reuters headline

Cultural Ambassador: A 21-year-old Welsh engineering student is recovering in a Cape Town, South Africa, hospital. The unnamed man ("He has requested that we do not give out any further information," a hospital spokeswoman says) was returning from a sightseeing trip to Stellenbosch when he got the idea to "moon" drivers on the highway out the back of the bus he was riding. He dropped his pants and pressed his buttocks against the back window. The window, which is also an emergency exit, swung right open. He tumbled out, landing on the highway with his trousers around his ankles, and skidded along the highway in front of astonished motorists. He was listed in serious condition with "severe abrasions and blood loss," but is expected to recover. (Reuters) ...*From his physical injuries, maybe.*

Hoop Dreams: Rickey Higgins, 17, a high school basketball player, was cited by police for an alcohol offense. Later he was convicted of drunk driving after he crashed his car into a tree. Warren Township (Ill.) High School said that was enough: he would not be allowed to play basketball for a year. Higgins now says he is an alcoholic, and alcoholism is a disability. Therefore, he says, he is being discriminated against and has filed a lawsuit under the Americans with Disabilities Act. Higgins hoped to get a college basketball scholarship, which is now at risk because he can't play. "This will definitely hurt that," he said. "I think I deserve a second chance." (AP) ...*Isn't that why the school waited until his second arrest?*

You've Got Male: Maricopa County, Ariz., Parks and Recreation Department office manager Susan Sousa sent an e-mail to her boss about various work-related issues. Rand Hubbell thought it looked interesting and forwarded it to his boss. Unfortunately, Hubbell didn't notice the P.S.: "Sometimes I will fantasize about ... our encounter the other evening. I'm getting aroused writing this," Sousa had added. Hubbell's boss noticed it. The county told

newspapers that Sousa and Hubbell will both be demoted for violating the county's e-mail policy. "I've learned a great deal from
it, obviously," Hubbell said. So will others: copies of the e-mails
will be used to train employees about e-mail rules. The publicity
has already resulted in both Sousa's and Hubbell's spouses finding out about their affair. (Arizona Republic) ...*Later, copies will
be used to train managers that public humiliation of employees
can lead to successful lawsuits.*

Keyboardrobics: Taking college courses over the Internet has
always had shortcomings. Malone College in Canton, Ohio, is
addressing one of them: the lack of physical education classes.
"I'm going to be like an online personal trainer," gushed Malone
track and field coach Charlie Grimes. The Personal Fitness class
provides three hours of credit, and will cost students $1,020. Will
online students actually work out? "As soon as the students leave
the classroom, I'm not sure what they're doing," Grimes admits.
(AP) ...*Wasting away their scholarship money.*

hguorhtkaerB: Researchers say they have found at least one of the
genes responsible for dyslexia. The research will provide "insight
into the nature and frequency of at least one gene that is involved
in reading and spelling," said Dr. Toril Fagerheim of University
Hospital of Tromsoe in Norway. He says the findings may help
diagnosis and treatment of the problem. (Reuters) ... *"It was right
there all the time," Fagerheim said. "I don't know why we didn't
see it before."*

Somebody Stop Me: Jimmy Haakansson, 39, charged with theft in
an unnamed city in Sweden, was given a chance to chat privately
with his lawyer. As two police officers guarding him waited in the
hall, Haakansson saw his opportunity: he jumped out the window
to escape. Unfortunately, the room was on the third floor, and he
ended up with a broken foot and back injuries. Haakansson is now
suing the state, saying the two officers should have prevented him
from jumping out the window. (AP) ...*And the police force is dis-
ciplining them for not putting him in a ninth floor conference
room.*

Bright Idea: Colin Humphreys of England's Cambridge University says he has improved on the light bulb. By adding gallium
nitride, "probably the most important new material since silicon,"
lights will burn brighter and use less electricity. And, he says,

"Because they last 10 years continuously, for a normal household operation they will effectively last a lifetime." (Reuters) ...*How many scientists did it take to change the light bulb?*

Full Circle: The "aggressive" San Diego, Calif., law firm Milberg Weiss Bershad Hynes & Lerach LLP recently sued Nintendo of America, Wizards of the Coast, and 4Kids Entertainment, charging that their sales practice of enticing children to buy Pokémon game cards constituted an illegal gambling scheme and racketeering. After filing the suit in a blaze of media coverage [*Poke the Man,* this volume, p41], Milberg Weiss realized that defendant 4Kids was the firm's own client. The firm has announced it will not only withdraw from the prosecution of the case, but will not defend 4Kids, either, since that could be a conflict of interest. (San Diego Union-Tribune) ...*Meanwhile, 4Kids has asked its corporate counsel to draw up a lawsuit against its lawyers for malpractice.*

No, Not "Firetruck": Leonard Carlo likes a particular word, and it's reflected in the decor of his Colorado Springs, Colo., bar. "F- - -ing Women" says the sign on the ladies room; "F- - -ing Men" it says on the opposite door. Another sign notes, "No f- - -ing tap or draw beer". A state liquor enforcement agent, noting a state regulation prohibiting profanity in bars, confiscated 29 signs. "The mother f- - -er came in like a German storm trooper," Carlo said. "He walked in my door and started ripping signs off my f- - -ing walls." The agent, however, left up Carlo's posting of the Ten Commandments and the U.S. Constitution. Carlo's liquor license is in danger of suspension, and he is suing, saying his free speech rights have been violated ("If you walk in and see 'f- - -' and you don't like it, get the f- - - out. There's 700 bars in town," he says.) Meanwhile, Carlo has had a message tattooed on his bald head which reads, "F- - - U. Leave me the f- - - alone." He challenged the agent, "Now, mother f- - - - -, take that one!" (Denver Post) ...*They will if they can.**

Four-Alarm Flannel: Firefighters in Chicago, Ill., are fuming over new department-issued pajamas. "If you're going to have a diverse fire department, where you have male and female firefighters sleeping in the same sleeping quarters, you have to do

* See photo and update at http://www.thisistrue.com/leonards.html

this," says Fire Cmdr. Willie Knight. Firefighters say they would rather the department bought them more safety equipment instead. The jammies are not flame retardant, so if they get a call in the middle of the night, the firefighters must put turnout coats over them. But Knight insists the nightclothes must be worn, since the department cannot afford separate sleeping quarters for female firefighters, and he wants to avoid sexual harassment lawsuits. "This is not a joke," Knight said. (UPI) ... *The public will be the judge of that.*

No, Really: War is Hell! The French Army reports that while they are not having any problems meeting recruitment goals, recent volunteers do not understand that armed combat can be dangerous. "Perhaps because of all the video games they ingurgitate, they don't seem to really link war and death," says Col. Alain Raevel, an aide to the Army chief General. (Reuters) ... *Warning: armed conflict may be dangerous to your health.*

Too Late, He Already Is
School Says Boy in Drag
Can't Be Queen
Reuters headline

I Dunno, What do You Wanna Do? Two 17-year-old cousins in Plymouth, Wis., wondered what it would be like to be shot. The two decided to shoot themselves to find out, until a 34-year-old relative stepped in and put a stop to it — by offering to do it for them. Each sought medical treatment after being shot in the leg, and the older man was arrested. (AP) ... *I wonder what it would be like to spend a decade in prison?*

Beat It: Researchers at the University of Sussex in England are developing "smart" pacemakers. Cardiologist Richard Vincent says that over time, pacemakers will "become more and more intelligent, more adaptive to a patient's lifestyle" and adjust their pacing parameters according to the users' needs. In addition, he says, the devices could be made with voice recognition features so, for instance, a heart patient could say aloud, "I'm going to walk up stairs" and the heart rate could adjust immediately.

(Reuters) ...*Great, until users forget themselves and yell at some-one to "Drop Dead!"*

Where Do You Want to Go Today? Author Kurt Vonnegut will talk about his work, but don't ask him to read it aloud. "I've never done a reading. It's the lowest art form imaginable," he sniffs. However, "I'll talk about stuff that bothers me, like the way people are being cheated out of the experience of 'becoming'. It's the computer which becomes now. People think, 'Oh, boy, wait until I get this new program.' Bill Gates will give you a program to write a perfect Shakespearean sonnet. For God's sake, that's not becoming." (AP) ...*Right. For that you need a high-speed connection to the 'net.*

I'll Wait: An unidentified 80-year-old man walking near his home in Summerton, N.C., was stopped by a man in a car with a knife who demanded money. The victim said he didn't have any money on him, but he did at home, so the robber offered to give him a ride. After arriving at his home, the victim went inside and called police as the robber waited in the car for him to bring out the cash. Police dispatchers could hear the robber impatiently honking his horn over the telephone. The car's 54-year-old driver was arrested and charged with kidnaping and attempted armed robbery. (The Sumter, S.C., Item) ...*The Bad News: robbers expect drive-up window service. The Good News: cops still pick up.*

Microeconomics: Nicaragua President Arnoldo Aleman praised his country's preliminary approval for entry into the World Bank and International Monetary Fund's Highly Indebted Poor Countries program. "We are beginning a new phase in our economic and social development, and when the process concludes, we will be free of our heavy debt," he proclaimed in a ceremony. How does a country celebrate their first step toward getting out of debt? The government decreed a half-day paid holiday for public and private workers to party. (Reuters) ...*The Bad News: There's a terrible financial problem. The Good News: We think we now understand why.*

To Sculpt and Preserve: "I can't understand what they are so upset about," says Rio de Janeiro, Brazil, plastic surgeon Luiz Fernando Dacosta. He has put up a billboard of a nude woman to showcase his surgical talents. "She shows off well the perfect lines of the human body, which is the major goal of plastic surgery," he said. But critics disagree. "Doctors have an obligation to be moderate and he was not," complained a spokesman for the Regional Council of Medicine. "A billboard of a nude woman like this exposes the whole medical establishment to ridicule." (Reuters) ...*Only because they can't make everyone look like that.*

Poof: Since 1977, wildland firefighters in the U.S. have been issued emergency shelters to shield them from burning to death if they become trapped by the forest fires they are fighting. But the aluminum-clad, tent-like shelters, which have been credited with saving 250 lives, apparently only protect from heat, not flame. U.S. Forest Service researchers have found that when flames touch the shelters, they "fill with highly flammable toxic smoke, which can ignite into a fireball." Researcher Leslie Anderson said "we've always said it's important to keep the shelter out of flames, and now we know why." (AP) ...*Apparently, it's similar in concept to giving spies cyanide capsules.*

Unclear Understanding: Convicted ax-murderer William "Cody" Neal is ready to face his punishment for killing three women in a bloody rampage. He told a panel of judges at his sentencing hearing in Golden, Colo., that he really would prefer not to be executed for his crimes, but if that's his sentence, so be it. "I want the responsibility for the whole thing," Neal told the court. "If I lose my life, I can live with that." (Denver Post) ...*And probably for longer than he thinks.*

Crime and Punishment II: Frank Darwin Alexander has pleaded guilty in federal court in Las Vegas, Nev., to three charges of attempted murder for mailing pipe bombs, including one addressed to President Clinton. But Alexander doesn't want to be homeless when he is let out of prison, so he has asked the judge to sentence him to life. "I'm 53," he said. "I can't see serving 40 years, coming out and living on the streets." The judge set sentencing for early next year. (AP) ...*It's nice to see people thinking ahead, planning for their retirement long before their productive years are over.*

Automated Service: Braulio Triano, a police officer patrolling Villahermosa, Tabasco, Mexico, checked the booth of an automatic teller machine at a bank and discovered a young couple inside. It was 2:00 a.m., and "We found them doing *that*," he said. "I couldn't believe it. I didn't know what to tell them. The first thing that occurred to me was to shout at them, 'What's going on?'" The woman explained: she was a prostitute. "He told me we were only going to withdraw money to go to a hotel," she said. (Reuters) ...*In a situation like that, withdrawal sounds like a pretty good plan.*

Deep Space Probe: Manned deep space missions would require spacecraft so large that fueling them becomes a problem. NASA, then, is studying the use of chemical modifications to onboard trash to generate propulsion. That, and the crew's excrement. "You can use human waste as well as other waste," said a spokesman. (Reuters) ...*Leading a future crewman to report, "I'm sorry, sir, but we only have enough fuel to reach Uranus."*

12-Click Program
Hooked on Internet?
Help Is Just a Click Away
Reuters headline

What Goes Up Must Come Down: Hilton Hotels Corp. is looking seriously at putting a hotel in Earth orbit. "We want to take a hard look at it and see if Hilton can be first into space," said company spokeswoman Jeannie Datz. But don't hold your breath: "It's certainly not going to happen tomorrow. We're talking 15 to 20 years down the road, if any of it makes sense." They have competition, too: California's Space Island Group also hopes to build an orbiting hotel. What might draw tourists to the expensive vacations? The view, certainly. But also, Space Island spokesman Gene Meyers adds, "What we've referred to as the romantic possibilities of zero gravity always comes up." (AP) ...*Nothing new: love and war have always been the main impetus behind technological innovations.*

A Kodak Moment: A man dropped off a roll of film to be developed at a Tesco supermarket in England. When store employees looked at the resulting prints, they recognized the men in the photos as the robbers who had raided the store two weeks before. Police pounced when Roland Tough, 22, came back to pick up his pictures. He had taken the photos of the gang and their loot to "show friends in prison how well they were doing." Tough has been sentenced to six years in prison for his part in the robbery. (London Times) ...*Shutterbug desperado stupidly submits snapshots to same store he assaulted, says snooping shop staff, so sharp constables snap on shackles and segregate scoundrel from society.*

Two-Fisted Drinker: A study by University of Kentucky nutritionist James Anderson shows that nursing raises a child's intelligence. "Our study confirms that breast-feeding is accompanied by about a five-points-higher IQ than in bottle-fed infants," Anderson said. He estimates that "maternal bonding and the decision to breast-feed account for about 40 percent of that increase," and "60 percent [is] related to the actual nutritional value of the breast milk." He adds that it takes at least eight weeks of breast-feeding to show any benefit. (AP) ...*Sorry, gentlemen: if you can read this, it's too late for you.*

Fixed Jury: William Woods was ready to begin trial in Ottawa, Ont., Canada, on charges of dangerous driving causing bodily harm. But the case had to be postponed because Woods was called for jury duty — for his own case. "Imagine the odds of it all," said his lawyer, Ken Hall. "He should have gone out and bought a lottery ticket." (Ottawa Citizen) ...*Or pled guilty and taken his chances on sentencing.*

Have a Seat: Scotland's Lord Doune, son of the 20th Earl of Moray, said in 1746 his ancestors loaned a chair from their castle to Bonnie Prince Charlie, who was on his way to fight the English in the Battle of Cullodon. It was never returned. Doune recently bought the chair back at auction from Sotheby's after it was found in southern England. It cost him 7,000 pounds (US$11,500). "We will be a bit more careful before we lend anything again," he said after returning the chair to the family's castle. (AP) ...*And still intact: the tag which reads "Do not remove this tag under penalty of beheading."*

Cutoff: Robbie Crawford wants to end road rage. The British computer consultant says demon drivers can be calmed by his rear-window electronic sign, which can flash messages such as "Thank You" and "Sorry" to other cars. He has manufactured 4,000 of the displays so far, betting his life savings that people will buy them. "I made a prototype of the device, I tried it out myself and found it really useful," he said. (Reuters) ...*A device that can be hacked to display "Back Off, Jerk!" is going to reduce road rage?*

Letter of Recommendation: Paul Converse, 47, graduated from law school at the University of South Dakota. He would like a license to practice law in Nebraska, but the Nebraska State Bar Commission will not allow him to take the bar exam. Why? Because Converse was constantly "abusive, disruptive, hostile, intemperate, intimidating, irresponsible, threatening or turbulent" during his school career, the Bar wrote in a rejection letter. (AP) ...*In most states, those are the minimum requirements for lawyers.*

Paging Dr. Welby: Americans get most of their information on health matters by watching daytime television, says U.S. Secretary of Health and Human Services Donna Shalala. She says a "failed edifice of science education" has resulted in a "scientifically illiterate" population. "We have college graduates who don't know the Earth orbits the sun in one year, or that dinosaurs lived before human beings," she said. So to help people learn, Shalala says she has instituted a program to send "accurate" health information to TV soap opera writers. (UPI) ...*And "accurate" dieting information to Oprah.*

Life Behind Bars: A day-long conference at the Smithsonian Institution recently honored the 25-year anniversary of the Universal Product Code. The standardized bar code on retail consumer products allowed stores to considerably speed up checkout by using laser scanners on approximately 5 billion items purchased per day worldwide. "In all my years, I've seen nothing that has changed the industry like the Universal Product Code," exclaimed Bob Martin, former president of Wal-Mart's international division. Some at the conference joked the bar code was the biggest innovation in supermarkets since sliced bread. (AP) ...*Which is also a random collection of thick and thin.*

Open Road: A Thai bus driver who made a fortune operating a fleet of luxury coaches now has his dream house. Samrauy Chuenchum's four million baht (US$98,000) house is shaped like a double-decker bus. The two-storey, two-bedroom house outside Bangkok is 62 feet long and 13 feet wide, and includes a simulator with steering wheel so the house can be "driven". His wife not only likes it, it was her idea. "He insisted on driving, and because he loved it so much, I told him to build our house like a bus," she said. She is also a bus driver. (Reuters) ...*Ralph Kramden, eat your heart out.*

Obviously, Not Very Well
Man Says Israeli Police Shot Him
AP headline

Bronco Busted: Nevada's Mustang Ranch is arguably the most famous brothel in the world. When the 440-acre ranch near Reno opened for business in 1955, prostitution was illegal, but it went legitimate in 1971 as the state's first modern legal bawdy house. Last summer, however, the federal government seized the property after its owners were found guilty of fraud and racketeering. The feds, not wanting to run a bordello, evicted the callgirls. The Bureau of Land Management has announced plans to turn it into a real ranch, and the home of its Wild Horse and Burro Adoption Center. (AP) ...*Thanks to the power of the federal government, you'll soon finally be able to get ass at the Mustang Ranch for free.*

Zap That Idea: "Old Sparky", the recently retired electric chair used by the State of Florida to put 238 inmates to death, will not be made available to museums for display, the Florida Department of Corrections has ruled after receiving requests from two museums. The chair, built by inmates in 1923, was taken out of service after flames shot out of the heads of two condemned men during their executions. DeVoe Moore, owner of the Tallahassee Antique Car Museum, wants to display the death chair. "If some of these kids could see the chair, or sit in it, look at it, their thoughts might change if they thought about putting on a trench coat, putting a gun under it and going out," he said. "It needs to be out there in a very tasteful manner." (Reuters) ...*As if that were possible.*

Taste for Death II: Thomas Provenzano was convicted in the murder of a courtroom bailiff in Orlando, Fla., 15 years ago and sentenced to death. But his execution was delayed after Provenzano proclaimed that he is Jesus Christ, indicating possible mental illness — or a clever ploy to postpone his death. State Rep. Howard Futch is angry about the delay. "Doesn't he think he's Jesus Christ or something?" Futch asked his colleagues. "Why don't we just crucify him? I'd make him a cross and we could take it out there to [death row] and nail him up." (Reuters) ...*Suddenly it becomes clearer where Floridians get their idea of "taste" when it comes to executions.*

See My Lawyer After Class: Robert McKillion, a computer teacher at Daphne High School in Daphne, Ala., has agreed not to charge students for using the restroom during class after a 14-year-old student wet his pants. "The teacher told him that he should have said it was an emergency," the boy's mother said. The kids had unanimously agreed to the fee to help pay for a party at the end of the semester, and the school's principal said the fee was "not required," but the county district attorney is investigating. "I don't believe you can take money from students to go to the bathroom, even if the payment is voluntary," he said. "I'm quite sure we could not treat prisoners that way." (AP) ...*No doubt, the headline on the story in the school paper was "District Attorney Affirms School Like Prison".*

School Discipline II: When Christopher Peregory, 12, was sent to the principal's office at Belle View Elementary School in Fairfax, Va., he decided instead to get out of town. The boy took the train to Reagan National Airport and slipped onto a TWA jetliner. Once he found himself in St. Louis, Mo., he panicked and called his mother. TWA, criticized for its lack of security or curiosity about a 12-year-old boy traveling alone, turned on the boy. "He did something wrong, he did something that was a violation of several statutes, and that should be the focus of what occurred here," an airline spokesman said. (AP) ...*That's just like a child to point to someone else and say "it wasn't me, he did it!"*

Paper or Plastic? Most robbers are prepared when they do their work. But a thief who hit a convenience store in St Petersburg, Fla., didn't have a disguise with him, so he grabbed a clear trash bag and pulled it over his head before approaching the clerk. "It looked like a big prophylactic down to his waist," a sheriff's spokesman said. "We got nice video from the store's camera." Herman Hill, 35, was caught nearby and arrested. (Reuters) ...*Sorry, pal: there's no such thing as safe robbery.*

Paper or Plastic? II: Jo Ann Walker had finished walking her dog at a park in Des Moines, Iowa. She put her bag on the trunk of her car as she was getting ready to leave when three teen-aged boys ran by, grabbed the bag, and called back to her, "Thank you!" As the polite thieves raced away, the only thing she could think of to say was "You're welcome!" The bag the boys had stolen contained her dog's droppings, which she had dutifully picked up behind him. "I just wish I could have seen their faces when they opened it up," she said. (AP) *...Or when they realize that they could still go to prison for stealing it.*

Numbskull: A test of more than 500 bank notes in London found that only four were free of measurable amounts of cocaine. "Once you've taken a snort, the compounds will be in the oils of your skin and get transferred to notes you handle," said Joe Reevy of Mass Spec Analytical, which conducted the test for the BBC. "That's the way the cocaine gets on to the notes." (Reuters) *...A statement which pretty much proves Joe Reevy isn't a drug user.*

New Fall Line: Fashion designer Paco Rabanne is sorry. When he heard the Russians planned to abandon the *Mir* space station, and then heard about the solar eclipse last August, he coupled those facts with his readings of Nostradamus and predicted *Mir* would crash into Paris on August 11, 1999, and completely destroy the city. Obviously, that didn't happen. "My analysis was wrong, completely wrong," he now says. "I made a massive mistake, a huge blunder, and now I publicly apologize." (AP) *...Anything in Nostradamus' writings that could be interpreted as an apology?*

Stretching the Merchandising Concept: The professional soccer team in Coventry, England, has announced it will offer an official condom. "This is not a joke product," said a spokesman. "We are a responsible club." (Reuters) *...Hopefully, not more than one player will need it at any one time.*

Twinkle, Twinkle Little Star

There May Be Diamonds in Planets

AP headline

Bread and Circuses: Thanks in part to the phenomenal success of the TV game show *Who Wants to Be a Millionaire?*, networks are scrambling to come up with new ideas — or reinventions of old ones — to grab a piece of the audience. CBS is trying the former with *Survivor*. The show will strand 16 Americans on an uninhabited island in the South China Sea. The last one to remain will win $1 million. "It's a double-edged sword," a gleeful CBS spokesman explained. "They need each other to survive, but they know only one can win." Cameras around the island will record their moves. The network expects a winner to emerge within seven weeks. (AP) ...*Gilligan's Island, The Next Generation.*

Bread and Circuses II: The Fox network, also wanting a chunk of the TV game show action, has announced *Greed.* Rushing it to air — Fox has ordered six episodes, even though it hasn't hired a host or finalized the format — the show is said to be modeled after *Family Feud,* except instead of families cooperating to win money, here the contestants will turn against each other for a chance at $2 million. (AP) ...*Coming soon from UPN:* Romans — *losers are fed to starving lions.*

Everyone Prefers Blondes: The North American ruddy duck, which spread to the British Isles about 50 years ago, is such an aggressive breeder that the European white-headed duck is in danger of extinction. "These ruddy ducks have a particular fancy for the European white-headed duck, mainly found in Spain," said a spokeswoman for English Nature, a government agency. Some fed-up environmentalists are backing the government's solution: the so-called "raping ducks" are being shot on sight. (Reuters) ...*If the problem was imported from America, it seems fitting that the solution also be.*

Adventures in Wildlife II: Fishermen are demanding that the New Mexico State Game and Fish Department do something about Lake Quemado. But even after removing about 45,000 goldfish from the lake, about 65,000 are still clogging the water, making it difficult to fish for more desirable species. The fish are thought to have bred from live bait dumped into the water. "When we got there I was shocked. The whole cove by the boat ramp was orange," says Ernest Jaquez, a state fisheries manager. He says the state will try less extreme options before draining or poisoning the lake, such as "training bass to eat the goldfish." (AP) ...*Or arming them with shotguns.*

Truth in Advertising: Two men from Georgia have been charged with violating the Bald and Golden Eagle Protection Act and the Migratory Bird Protection Act. Leighton Deming, 56, and Thomas Marciano, 42, were arrested by the FBI after trying to sell an apparently genuine turn-of-the-century eagle-feathered head-dress worn by Apache leader Geronimo. The FBI was alerted to the scheme by the advertisement itself, which was posted on the Internet. "It said 'only serious candidates must respond because it is illegal to sell eagle feathers in the United States'," an FBI spokeswoman said. (Reuters) ...*Everyone is entitled to be stupid now and then, but some people really abuse the privilege.*

Pre-Qualified for Congress: The same day University of Missouri-St. Louis students elected Darwin Butler, 35, student body president, Darwin pleaded guilty to two felony theft charges. Students are now upset that their representative hid the charges from them. But "It was none of their business," Butler said afterward, defending keeping his legal problems under his hat. "And you never know, there's 12,000 students [here]," he said. "I can't be the only one who done something." Should a felon represent others? "Criminals run this country, criminals always," he said. "When those three boats came over, one of the boats had criminals on it." (AP) ...*Ah yes: the Nina, the Pinta and the Botany Bay.*

He's Probably Turning in His Grave: Catholic priest Fr. Marcelo Rossi of Rio de Janeiro, Brazil, has worshipers dancing in their pews. His new CD of aerobics music is at the top of Brazilian charts thanks to "Vira de Jesus" ("Jesus Twist"). In the country's 1991 census, 83 percent of Brazil's population described themselves as Catholic, but only 15 percent of those said they went to Mass regularly. But Fr. Rossi holds his Mass in soccer stadiums to accommodate the crowds of young people who wish to attend. (Reuters) ...*Why should the devil get all the good music?*

Tick Tock: The United States Postal Service installed tens of thousands of "countdown clocks" in post offices all over the country showing the number of days, hours, minutes and seconds until the year 2000. But some post offices in Texas and California have removed the clocks after customer complaints — and noticing a downward trend in customer satisfaction surveys. "We have

40,000 post offices nationwide," a USPS spokesman said. "Try as we might to please everyone, there's always going to be something that offends some people." The postmaster of Colleyville, Texas, said patrons said the clocks "made them feel hurried, like their lives are going too fast." (AP) ...*More likely they simply realized their waiting time in line was being measured in days.*

Point of View: What is the "Medical Miracle of the Century"? It depends on who you ask. A British research group asked doctors. Aspirin was chosen as the greatest medical advance of the century by cardiologists, chemotherapy by oncologists, antidepressants by psychiatrists, and penicillin by doctors in general practice. (Reuters) ...*While lawyers cited million-dollar malpractice insurance policies as the greatest achievement of medicine.*

It's Difficult to Say "Duh" with Your Mouth Full

Study: Obesity Can Shorten Lifespan

AP headline

History Lesson: Georgia School officials are aghast that the classic painting of "Washington Crossing the Delaware" in a fifth-grade textbook shows George Washington's pocket watch lying on his thigh. Dirty-minded school administrators think it looks like the president's genitalia arc on display. "I know what it is and I know what it is supposed to be," insists the superintendent of Muscogee County schools, but he and the principal of Due West Elementary School agree that when it comes to fifth-graders, "it would make their year" if they thought they were peeking into the president's pants. So prim paternalists purged the presumed presidential phallus from textbooks all over the state — by tearing the page out. (AP) ...*When you get right down to it, nothing much has changed in presidential politics over the centuries.*

Those Who Ignore History Are Doomed to Flunk It: Officials at Nevis (Minn.) High School are refusing to allow a photo of student Samantha Jones into the school yearbook since it shows the senior, who is joining the Army after graduation, posing with a decommissioned 155 mm howitzer cannon on display outside the local Veterans of Foreign Wars post. "Whether it's in military, recreational or sporting form, anything shaped like a gun or knife is banned" from school under the district's "zero tolerance" weapons policy, explained Superintendent Dick Magaard. The school board deadlocked on a vote whether to overturn the ban, even after the board chairman pointed to war photos hanging on the school's walls. "I back my daughter 100 percent on this," Samantha's mother told the school board. "The lawyer will be sending you papers." (AP) ...*It's no use: school officials cannot be paper trained.*

Modern History: British schoolchildren are a little unclear about the roles of authority figures in their lives. Children interviewed for a documentary on BBC television believe Queen Elizabeth "sits around drinking wine all day," while others confuse Prime Minister Tony Blair with God. Blair "has got grey long hair, curly with a grey beard, a grey-like dressy thing and he does miracles," a young girl explained. (Reuters) ...*Politicians don't perform miracles, they just take credit for them.*

Ancient History: Oedipus, the mythological Greek figure known for killing his father and marrying his mother, should probably be known for something more common, argues Robert Allen, editor of *Pocket Fowler's Modern English Usage*: road rage. That's right, he says, road rage is not a modern phenomenon. "It actually dates back to the second millennium B.C.," Allen asserts, when "Oedipus killed his father at a crossroads when they got in each other's way." Authorities say "road rage" has led to an increase in vehicular violence and crashes. (Reuters) ...*Which will in future be known as Oedipus Wrecks.*

Take Two Irish Coffees and Call Me in the Morning: Researchers at the University of Texas in Houston have been testing various substances known to affect the brain in hopes of finding a treatment to limit the damage of cerebral strokes. The most effective so far: a shot of booze with a coffee chaser. "We found that if we gave a combination of alcohol and caffeine, equivalent to, say, one drink of alcohol and two or three cups of coffee, that there's almost complete protection from a stroke," said study leader James Grotta, a neurologist. But care must be taken. "If you give too much of either the alcohol or the caffeine, then the effect is lost," Grotta warned. Worse, "if you give the combination chronically — for a week or so prior to the stroke — there's also no benefit." (Reuters) ... *The paradox: even if it doesn't work, you'll still feel better.*

Serial Criminal: Prosecutors say when Penny Page got mad, she got even. She was upset with a job counselor, a landlord, and a neighbor, so she signed them up for a total of 350 magazine subscriptions. "You're a menace to society and to yourself," ruled Painesville, Ohio, Judge Paul Mitrovich, finding Page guilty of forgery. She was sentenced to two months in jail, three years of probation, and must attend an anger management class. (AP) *...And she was ordered to cancel the judge's new subscription to* Prison Penpals Weekly.

In the Pink: Police in Manchester, England, have cautioned an 83-year-old man after he admitted he forged a prescription for Viagra so that he could keep up with his 39-year-old girlfriend. "The police were very nice about it," Ernest Pink said afterward. (Reuters) *...Of course: they regard him as a role model.*

Light it Up: Cigarette maker Philip Morris wants the public to know that ...*well*... it does a lot more than make cigarettes. A new $100 million ad campaign will remind consumers that the company also owns such brands as Miller Brewing, Jell-O, Maxwell House coffee and Oscar Mayer bologna, and that a fraction of corporate profits go to good causes. Steven Parrish, the company's senior vice president for corporate affairs, says the company has tired of "the most extreme of our critics" and hopes the company's "demonization can end or at least fall on increasingly deaf ears." The ads will carry the new slogan, "Working to Make a Difference. The people of Philip Morris." (AP) *...After the company rejected "Philip Morris: Inducing cancer worldwide was just the beginning."*

All Shook Up: A recent auction of various Elvis Presley belongings brought plenty of bidders. A wristwatch brought $36,875, a humidor $28,750. Then the auctioneers brought out Elvis' TV antenna, which had accidentally been shipped with items to be sold. They put it on the block, and it was quickly bid up to $1,725. "It's a real piece of Graceland, not just some document," said buyer Sue Fergerstrom of Springfield, Mo. "And when he tries to contact me, I'll have better reception." (AP) *...Except when he calls, you'll be watching* Laverne and Shirley.

Everybody Needs a Hobby

Why Americans Love to Hate Government

Reuters headline

Police Story: The New York City Police Department says tourists are increasingly trying to take advantage of the system by filing false reports of being robbed in order to collect on travel insurance. Visitors are coming in with tall tales — and are increasingly being charged with filing false police reports, which is punishable by $1,000 fines and up to four years in prison. One tourist told the cops he was "robbed in broad daylight surrounded by hundreds of people," says Capt. James O'Neill of the Central Park Precinct. That report "really had cops rolling their eyes." One thing that tips officers off, he says, is that tourists "give us a Hollywood version. Something corny, like the perp said, 'Stick 'em up'. Nobody says that anymore." (AP) *...You mean cops still say "perp"?*

A Moment in History: Kevin Warwick, head of cybernetics at England's Reading University, was on his way to exhibit British technology to Russian scientists. But British Airways refused to let him board his flight because animals are not allowed in the cabin. Warwick explained that his 10,000 pound (US$16,000) cat was a robot — the technology he was going to demonstrate in Russia — "but they were adamant that the robot would have to go in the hold because of their rules about animals," he said. He flew out on another airline rather than risk his robot in the cargo hold. (London Evening Standard) *...Making 1999 the year that bigotry and discrimination against cyborgs first reared its ugly head.*

Compare and Contrast: An English teacher in Franklin, Ohio, assigned an essay to her students: "If you had to assassinate one famous person who is alive right now, who would it be and how would you do it?" An alternative question: who should live "if you had to lose everyone you know in a tragic accident except one person"? Franklin High School Principal Robert Leahy refuses to identify the teacher, but says he told her the essay topics were "inappropriate" and will take no further action. (AP) *...While any kid who learns from this example is destined for jail.*

Compare and Contrast II: A 13-year-old boy in Ponder, Texas, assigned to write a "Halloween horror story" for school, followed the instructions well. The boy's mother said he got an "A" on the essay, plus extra credit for reading it aloud to his class. The unnamed student's one-paragraph, misspelling-laden essay tells of a haunted house where "I busted out with a 12 guage [*sic*] and Ismael busted out with 9 mm" and shot two classmates trying to scare them — and "I acssedently [*sic*] shot Mrs. Henry," the teacher. School officials found the essay "disturbing" and called police, who came to the school and arrested the boy. He remained in custody charged with "making terroristic threats" for five days, until bad publicity forced county officials to drop the charge and release him. (Reuters) ...*Yet another successful appeal to the Court of Public Opinion.*

Pop Quiz: Making a campaign stop in Boston, Mass., presidential hopeful George W. Bush was stumped when a local TV reporter asked him a few questions. Who are the leaders of Pakistan, India, Taiwan and Chechnya? Bush got "Lee" for Taiwan, and couldn't answer the others at all. "Wait. Wait. Is this 50 questions?" he asked, stalling for time, and later called the questions "gotcha journalism." Bush had previously referred to Greeks as "Grecians" and Kosovars as "Kosovoians," so he was supposed to be ready with an answer to questions he didn't know: "Americans don't expect their presidential candidates to be trivia experts; they want a leader who has a clear vision for America's future." But he apparently forgot his prepared comeback. (AP) ...*Bring back Ronald Reagan. He could remember his lines.*

Pop Quiz II: Emboldened by the headlines made when G.W. Bush couldn't come up with the right answers to trivia questions, a reporter gave President Bill Clinton a math question on a slip of paper: "If there are three cucumbers in a pound, and Burger King buys 3.2 million pounds of pickles. And you can cut 20 slices of pickle from each cucumber, how many pickle slices will you get?" And, while he was at it, who is the leader of Chechnya? Clinton considered the problem for a moment and wrote "192 million" on the paper, adding "I checked the calculation with the Chechnyan leader Aslan Maskhadov and he agrees." (AP) ...*It's no wonder Americans don't respect reporters. We don't care how* *many theoretical pickles are in a pound, we want to know what Washington is going to do about the deficit.*

Quite: British language purists are shocked that the bible of good English speech, *Fowler's Modern English Usage*, has come out in favor of American English. "It is linguistically misconceived and historically unjustified to regard the American influence on English as necessarily harmful," argues editor Robert Allen. He says American is "rich" and, thus, its "influence on British English in recent years has been enriching rather than a threat." The "old school" of proper English seems to think Americanisms are leading to a "moral decline" in Britain, but Allen argues the opposite, noting that insensitive words such as "cripple" for the disabled and "dumb" for those unable to speak are now "virtually outlawed" in the U.S. (Reuters) *...Just so: without American influence, Britons might be speaking German now.*

Slave to Fashion

Platform Shoes
Claim Another Life

Reuters headline

Quit Saying I'm Violent or I'll Kill You: Students at the University of Colorado in Boulder rioted recently. Again. The recent melee — "the fourth time in three years students took to the streets to riot," university regent Jim Martin says — caused $100,000 in damage. "Where should this $100,000 come from? It shouldn't come from the taxpayers." Martin has proposed a solution: make students pay for riot damage with a student fee, just like the fees charged to support student activities and clubs. Student leaders, however, say that if such a fee is enacted, it will cause a riot. (Denver Post) *...The old "I don't want to belong to a club that would accept me as a member" syndrome.*

Public Health Threat: Professor of public health Alexander Wagenaar of the University of Minnesota wondered how easy it is for drunks to get more alcohol, so he hired actors posing as "obviously intoxicated tipplers" and sent them to 336 bars and stores to buy more booze. They were able to make purchases 79 percent of the time. "Intoxicated bar patrons are at very high risk for causing alcohol-related injury to themselves and others," Wagenaar said. "What this tells us is that there is an urgent need for additional enforcement of laws prohibiting sales to intoxicated patrons." (Reuters) ...*Either that, or he needs to hire much better actors.*

Social Security: A survey by the Consumer Federation of America has found that 28 percent of Americans agree that winning a lottery or sweepstakes is their "best chance to obtain a half a million dollars or more in your lifetime." However, the Federation notes, by merely saving $50 a week in a savings account earning a 9 percent annual yield, the savings would grow to well over a million dollars in 40 years. The odds of winning the lottery are 1 in several million. The odds of being struck by lightning are significantly more likely — about 1 in 600,000. (AP) ...*And the odds of losing at least a third of any big winnings to taxes are about 1 in 1.*

Against the Odds II: Anuban Bell, 24, and Sunee Whitworth, 39, were struck by lightning in Hyde Park in London, England. Underwires in their support bras conducted the electrical charges straight to their hearts, killing them instantly. "This is only the second time in my experience of 50,000 deaths where lightning has struck the metal in a bra causing death," said coroner Paul Knapman at an inquest. (Reuters) ...*Quick: Buy a lottery ticket.*

You Haven't Got a Prayer: Researchers at the Mid America Heart Institute in Kansas City, Mo., say their study shows that heart patients who had strangers praying for them had fewer complications than those who didn't. "It's potentially a natural explanation we don't understand yet," said study lead William Harris. Or, "it's potentially a super- or other-than-natural mechanism." Other researchers urged caution, since most such studies are eventually proven flawed, since they don't account for the "non-prayed-for" group's family, which might be praying for them, or because they don't equally group the patients and controls according to gender, level of disease, or other factors. And some studies have actually shown the prayed-for are worse off. (AP) ...*Whether it works or not, it's about the only thing insurance covers these days.*

Think Outside the Box: Jun Sato, 25, could not find work in downtown Tokyo, Japan, so he made up his own job. Dressed in protective padding, he lets people on the street don boxing gloves and beat him for three minutes for 1,000 yen (US$10). "I enjoy being used as a punching bag," he says. "It's... another way to experience life. I want to continue as long as my body holds up." (Reuters) ...*Most people just call that "marriage".*

May it Please the Court: Frances and Harold Mountain divorced four months ago, but couldn't agree on how to split their Beanie Baby collection, valued at up to $5,000. Exasperated Las Vegas, Nev., Family Court Judge Gerald Hardcastle ordered that all the stuffed toys be brought into the courtroom, and then watched as Frances, then Harold, took turns choosing one of the Beanies at a time. "It's ridiculous and embarrassing," Frances said before diving straight for "Maple the Bear" as her first pick. (AP) ...*The judge also granted her request to go back to her maiden name, Molehill.*

More Love and Marriage: Thomas Rossi testified in court that he and his wife Denise had been so happy, "we even shared the same electric toothbrush." But three years ago, Denise won $1.3 million in the lottery. She did not tell him about the win, but instead filed for divorce. His lawyer said "it was pure serendipity that he found out" about it when the lottery commission sent her a letter to his address two years later. He didn't get mad, he got even: a Los Angeles, Calif., judge has awarded Thomas all of Denise's lottery winnings, ruling that she "acted out of fraud or malice" in concealing the money during the divorce proceedings, contrary to the state's community property laws. (Reuters) ...*Watch out for lightning, honey.*

Just Add Water: Thanks to "recent breakthroughs" in genetic research, within 25 years it may be possible to grow artificial replacement genitals for people. "As unbelievable as this may be, ...production of functioning human organs such as the penis and vagina are being done today in the laboratory," says Dr. Myron Murdock, national director of the Impotence World Association. Someday, he says, they could be "surgically implanted to produce a functioning, erogenous sexual organ." (Reuters) ...*Why wait 25 years? Viagra is artificially growing sex organs today.*

Prices are Heating Up: The Coca-Cola Co. is testing vending machines that can automatically raise prices when the weather gets hotter. When demand for a cold drink rises because of heat, "it is fair that it should be more expensive," argues Coke chairman M. Douglas Ivester. But company spokesman Rob Baskin, asked if customers might object to such price rises, insists the company will not be using such machines "anytime soon, if ever," adding "You could probably make a vending machine that could fly, too, but I don't think we would do that." (AP) ...*Unless that would increase their profit by a penny a can.*

Especially Now

Collapsed Bridge in China Faulty
AP headline

Status Symbol: Cadillac says its average buyer is now 65, so it is trying to entice younger people to buy its luxury cars and reverse a two-decade slide in sales. To do that, it has announced a new ad campaign dubbed "The Power of &" — a theme that pairs opposites which might attract buyers: night & day. Stars & stripes. Man & woman. The ampersand is used "in an effort to get attention and suggest that a combination often creates something bigger than the sum of the parts." (AP) ...*But the younger generation realizes that's just not where it's @.*

Get a Room: Tapachula, Mexico, prison warden Raul Zarate Diaz apparently liked to peek at inmates having sex with their wives during visits. He was discovered when he crashed through a skylight over the conjugal visitation section in his prison, falling 23 feet and landing next to a prisoner and his wife in bed. Diaz, who was found with a porn magazine — and a pair of binoculars for closer looks — was killed by the fall. (Reuters) ...*See? You don't always go blind first.*

Ayerhead: Emmett Ayers II, 20, needed to drop by the sheriff's department in Moulton, Ala., to pick up his driver's license, which had earlier been confiscated by deputies. Since he didn't have his driver's license with him, and didn't want to get in trouble for driving his car to the station without it, he had his nephew drive instead. His nephew is 4 years old. Deputies who witnessed the boy drive into the parking lot arrested Ayers and charged him with three misdemeanors: allowing a minor to drive, reckless endangerment and failing to have the boy strapped into a child seat. (AP) ...*Plus a felony: negligent thinking.*

Help Wanted: The *Wall Street Journal,* the *New York Times* and other newspapers have rejected an ad which features a picture of President Clinton pumping gas with the caption, "What are you gonna do now, Bill?" The ad, for Utah-based job referral company myjobsearch.com, "was not intended to be a slam on anybody," said company president Heather Stone. "It is a fact of life that he is going to be making a career transition." She said she was told by the newspapers the ad was "not in good taste", but is philosophical about the rejection, since myjobsearch.com doesn't accept all ads either. "I have my criteria. Obviously, the *New York Times* has its." (Salt Lake Tribune) ...*Unfortunately, Bill doesn't have his.*

Get Serious: Billionaire Donald Trump wants to be taken seriously in his bid for president. "I think I'm taken seriously. A lot of people are saying so and I can tell," he insists, dismissing political poll results which show he hardly exists. He says he knows voters take him seriously because when he appears on talk shows, the shows get high ratings. "Geraldo Rivera says I'm a hot guest," he gushed. (AP) ...*Making Trump the first person to take Geraldo seriously.*

Moove Along: So many motorists were concerned that a cow walking in knee-deep water in a flooded field was stuck that it caused a traffic jam near De Bary, Fla. To get traffic moving again — and to stop 911 calls to the Highway Patrol about a "drowning" cow — highway workers set up an electronic sign to flash the message "The Cow is OK" to passing cars. But two days later, the sign was still there, causing a traffic jam as motorists looked for the cow, which had long since walked away. (Reuters) ...*These are the same drivers, of course, who would never stop to help an injured person.*

Opportunity Only Knocks Once: Most people think good doors will stop burglars. One burglar, however, stopped at the door. Police in Cleveland, Ohio, have arrested David Lee Johnson, 35, and charged him with stealing the doors off 19 homes. Most of the doors were sculpted with elaborate designs and worth $500 to $2,000 each. Police say the arrest ended a six-week string of door thefts. "Haven't had a door stolen since," a police investigator said. "Knock on wood." (AP) ...*Now Johnson will get a chance to touch iron.*

There Are No Absolutes: It's all right to laugh at other people's problems. Duesseldorf, Germany, psychoanalyst Claudia Sies says *schadenfreude* (joy over someone else's misfortune) is actually healthy, since it "relieves stress because it can lead to a hearty laugh that helps people relax." Targets of the laughter, she says, should just laugh along with them. (Reuters) ...*On the other hand, when she presented her theory to the Deutsche Freudian Society, they laughed her out of the room.*

Defrost Cycle: The U.S. Congress has taken the first step to preserve a Minuteman nuclear missile silo in South Dakota and turn it into a Cold War museum. The Minuteman "was America's first push-button nuclear missile," says South Dakota Sen. Tim Johnson, who sponsored legislation to spend $5 million to preserve silos at Ellsworth Air Force Base. "When the wing was deactivated, something was missing on the high plains of western South Dakota," agrees Rep. John Thune of the same state, adding that under one missile's concrete door, which resembles a pizza box, "someone wrote, 'Worldwide delivery in 30 minutes or less or your next one is free.' Dark humor, I know, but it was a reality." (AP) ...*Opening soon: The Museum of Geopolitical Insanity.*

Another Great Leap in Dieting Science

More Exercise May Help Weight Loss

AP headline

Put a Lid on It: Santa Fe, N.M., Municipal Judge Frances Gallegos likes to sentence minor offenders to community service, but with a twist: while doing the work, the offenders must wear color-coded hats. Domestic violence convicts get blue hats, shoplifters green, drunk drivers pink. "There isn't a single high school kid or even a grade school kid in this town that doesn't know what the pink hat is all about," Gallegos says. And one more color has recently been added: people who don't clean up after their dogs are now assigned brown hats. (AP) ... *While the wrongly convicted get white hats.*

A Girl's Best Friend: A clerk at a jewelry store inside the Caesars Palace casino in Las Vegas, Nev., said Lori Carroll, 32, asked to see a one-carat diamond ring. He handed it over ...and it immediately disappeared. Police searched her, but didn't find it, so she was taken to a hospital and X-rayed. Sure enough, police say, she had swallowed it. Carroll was charged with burglary, grand larceny and possession of stolen property, and the $4,000 ring "reappeared" in the jail's medical ward 10 days later. "We went down and identified" it, the store manager said. "It still had our price tag on it." (AP) ... *Ten days? Lori, you're eating the wrong kind of carrots.*

Should Auld Acquaintance Be Forgot: What are your plans for New Year's eve? Britain's Health Education Authority publicly urged "young people to prepare now" by buying condoms to take with them when they go out to celebrate the end of the 1900s. Good timing: two weeks later, a survey by British condom-manufacturer Durex found that about half of the world's youth hope to celebrate the dawn of the year 2000 by having sex. After the fireworks are over, 60 percent of British youth, aged 16–21, hope to end the night with a ...*um*... bang, and 17 percent of virgins hope to lose their innocence that night. (Reuters, 2) ...*On the other hand, most people fail to keep their new year's resolutions.*

Shaken, Not Stirred: San Francisco, a bit envious of New York City's giant dropping "ball" to signal the arrival of the new year, is hoping to steal some attention by dropping a 10-foot "olive" into a seven-storey-tall martini on Union Square at midnight on December 31. "This is going to put San Francisco on the map as the 'Big Olive', just as New York is the 'Big Apple'," said a spokeswoman for the St. Francis Hotel, which is behind the stunt. But the Rev. Cecil Williams, who has plans for an open-air prayer vigil on Union Square, is aghast. "Is this the kind of message to be sending on the new millennium?" he asked, adding the spectacle will be a "distraction" from his services. But the St. Francis defends its plans. "We are entirely respectful of the interfaith community, but we feel that the martini is an icon of today's world," their spokeswoman said. (Reuters) ...*In a brilliant publicity stunt, at dawn Alka Seltzer will drop in two giant tablets.*

Pyramid Power: Egyptian authorities say the coming of the millennium is attracting a large number of "pilgrims" to the Great Pyramid of Giza. "The pyramids carry the consciousness, the constant of light," says Chalanda Ma, a California "guru" leading tour groups to the pyramids. Giza plateau director Zahi Hawass says most of the pilgrims are fine, but "there are those who really are nuts, fill the Internet with lies and think we are hiding evidence about the lost civilization" of pyramid builders. "The Pyramidiots want to steal the pyramids for themselves," he says. Perhaps thinking about the 3,600 Egyptian pounds (US$1,052) groups pay to enter the structures, he quickly added, "But I don't mean that those who meditate inside the Pyramids are Pyramidiots. They are nice people and they should be respected." (Reuters) ...*At least until their checks clear.*

Thwarted by Technology: Police in Reno, Nev., were hot on the trail of a convenience store robber, but despite aid from a helicopter with a spotlight, they couldn't find him in a residential neighborhood. Until exactly 4:00 a.m. "After two hours of searching, an officer heard a beeping alarm," a police spokesman said. The officer, standing at the foot of a 40-foot spruce tree, heard a watch alarm beeping in the tree. "Another officer started going up the tree with a flashlight and saw the guy's foot." Carlos Herrera, 40, was pulled down and charged with robbery, and is a suspect in three other robberies earlier that night. (AP) ...*And, apparently, he had an appointment for another.*

Housing Boom: The Los Angeles Sheriff's Department said they had permission from the property owners — the California Department of Transportation — to set off a bomb in a vacant house in La Verne, Calif., as a training exercise. But Caltrans says no, they didn't actually own the house yet, as their purchase was still in escrow. And even if they did own it they didn't grant anyone permission to blow it up, a spokesman said. The SWAT team's bomb tore a hole in a wall, broke 11 windows, and threw cinder blocks around, causing considerable damage — enough that Caltrans has canceled its purchase contract on the property. Meanwhile, neighbors are angry they weren't notified before the exercise, and so is the La Verne police department: they made an emergency response to the explosion, since they weren't notified of the exercise either. (Pasadena Star-News) *...Suburban renewal, Los Angeles style.*

Somehow, It Figures
Bible Belt Leads U.S. in Divorces
AP headline

Every Performance, the Same Newspaper Review — "It Stinks": Shakespeare is in the toilet. No, really. The Bog Standard Theatre Company in Malvern, England, spent three years converting an old restroom building into a 12-seat theater. "Shakespeare said all the world's a stage so I guess that includes toilets," a company spokesman said. However, "ironically we don't have room for a loo." (Reuters) *...To pee or not to pee. That is the question.*

He May be Lying: A good lie is getting harder to find. So says John Soeth, president of the Burlington, Wis., Liars Club. He says that their annual contest is bringing in fewer tall tales than usual, and that concerns him. "If lying goes away, what's left in America?" he asks. Perhaps the problem is that professionals are not eligible. "Our club is only open for amateurs. The politicians can't join," he says. "If politicians were included, the average person would not know what to do." (AP) *...Pretty much the same way that if honest people were elected, politicians wouldn't know what to do.*

Mummy Dearest: Robert Horton posted $170 in bail to get his wife Belinda out of jail. Wanting to make sure she made her court appointment so he wouldn't lose the bail money, the Phoenix, Ariz., man bound her up, including her mouth, with a roll of duct tape and delivered her to the Maricopa County Superior Court. "He said something like, 'Here she is'," a sheriff's spokesman said. Witnesses said she "looked like a mummy". A fire department rescue crew was called to extricate her. "She was obviously very angry," a fire official said. "She would wince every once in a while, but she didn't say one word to our guys." (Reuters, AP) *...Of course not: they were smart enough to leave her mouth for last.*

With This Ring: When Rodger Lindh broke up with his fiancée, Janis Surman, he asked for his $21,000 engagement ring back. Surman refused. The Pennsylvania couple's fight for the ring not only went into the courts, the case made it all the way to the state's Supreme Court. The seven-judge panel ruled that since Pennsylvania is a "no-fault divorce" state, "similar principles" should be applied to broken engagements. Surman was ordered to return the ring to Lindh. The court battle took six years. (AP) *...Which is probably longer than the marriage would have lasted.*

Don't Worry, Be Happy: David Blanchflower of New Hampshire's Dartmouth College and Andrew Oswald of the U.K.'s University of Warwick studied 100,000 people to see how happy they were. They found that happiness is lowest around age 40, and then goes up after that, and that a lasting marriage brought as much happiness as an additional $100,000 in yearly income. (Reuters) *...Whereas a divorce brings as much sadness as losing $100,000, especially since both usually happen at the same time.*

Fringe Benefits: Chris Reece, 20, said he applied for the job on a dare. But he got it, and is now a salesman at the Victoria's Secret lingerie store in Medford, Ore. "I'm not going to lie to you," he admits, "it's a prime opportunity to meet a girl there." But first, he gets to take home samples of the store's products. Though he doesn't plan to use them himself. "I was talking to my Mom, and she told me her bra size. I don't want to know this." (AP) *...If he were really qualified for the job, he'd already have known.*

Your Wish is My Command: When clerk Lee Johnson of the Li'L Cricket store in Spartanburg, S.C., was robbed, he hit the silent alarm. When he saw a car arrive out front, he saw it was a sheriff's deputy responding to the alarm. Apparently the robber didn't notice who drove up, so Johnson asked if he could go out and tell the arriving "customer" the store was closed. Sure, the robber said. Johnson went to the door and let the deputy in to arrest Kim Meredith, 34, who was charged with armed robbery. "This man needs to be on dumb crook news," Johnson told reporters. (AP) *...Granted.*

Pop Goes the Weasel: There are some pretty silly things on the Internet. One of the silliest now has a soundtrack. The "Hamster Dance" site on the World Wide Web has spawned "The Hamster Song" by the Cuban Boys, who are not Cuban and are not all boys.

It has become one of the most-requested songs on British radio —
thanks to an Internet-based publicity campaign. "I like the hamster record," says British pop music commentator Charles Shaar
Murray. "There is something eloquent in its sheer vacuity. At
least this gives us the chance — if Y2K is going to give us a mil-
lennial apocalypse — to at least sink giggling insanely into the
abyss." (Reuters) *...Yes, but why go out with a whimper when one
can go out with a bang?*

Remedial Administration: Officials of the Los Angeles Unified
School District have decided to keep the practice of "social promotion" in place, even though they had planned to stop it this
year. The concept allows students to graduate to the next grade
level, even when they have failing grades, so they can be in the
same grade as the rest of their age group. Had the district, the largest in California, dropped the scheme as scheduled, approximately 350,000 of their 711,000 students would have to be held
back next year. (AP) *...Thus keeping them pretty much in the same
grade as the rest of their age group.*

Talisman Tailgating: A survey by Britain's Automobile Association found that some beginning drivers bring rather unusual good
luck charms with them when they take their driving exams. Some
prefer religious relics, of course. Others, presumably women,
wear special red bras. Several report taking "odd" shoes. And
then there's toenail clippings. "It is perfectly acceptable if you
believe a box of toenail clippings will help," said a reassuring AA
spokeswoman. (Reuters) *...Sure, lady: you're not the one who has
to hold them.*

Except Footprints
Police Search Home 300 Times, Find Nothing
Reuters headline

Final Call for Boarding: The operator of the Malpensa Airport in
Milan, Italy, has announced a free ice rink for passengers to skate
away their waiting time at the airport. The airport, known for its
long delays, will offer skates for rent. Meanwhile, a new attrac-

tion has also been announced for Amsterdam's Schiphol Airport in the Netherlands. The Yam Yum Caviar Club, a chain of brothels, plans to open a bordello in the airport's departure area. Prostitution is legal in the Netherlands, and government officials are reportedly "receptive" to the plan. "Passengers will be treated to a luxury welcome with champagne and caviar and can opt for a relaxing massage," a spokesman for the brothel said. "They could pop in before going home to the lady wife." (Reuters, 2) ...*No, really, dear: those marks are from the skates.*

Mission Impossible: Police in DeKalb, Ill., have arrested a man for trying to burglarize the police station, officers say. "We usually don't have people breaking in [here]. That's pretty rare," said Lt. Jim Kayes. John M. Lu, 22, was allegedly crawling through the ceiling of the station toward the evidence locker after entering through a window. Officers heard him and pulled him down. Police had arrested him less than 24 hours earlier for secretly videotaping women in a dressing room and had confiscated his camera. "He wanted his camera and the tape back," Kayes said, adding that after Lu attempted suicide following his second arrest, he was taken to a hospital for a psychiatric examination. (AP) ...*Sounds like he needed that long before he attempted suicide.*

Step On In: Genuflex, a Venice, Italy, manufacturer of confessional booths, has unveiled its new "state-of-the-art" confessional. The 12 million lire (US$6,250), walnut-finished booth shows whether it is occupied or vacant. It includes black leather seating and soundproofing, and can be equipped with an optional "hygienic filter" between the priest and penitent. But "the real novelties of the confessional," says Genuflex, are its built-in heating and air-conditioning systems. (Reuters) ...*The "real novelty" being the priest's ability to quickly heat up the booth to warn about perils of hell.*

See Ya Sheila: When Australia's official women's soccer team issued a calendar featuring the players posing in the nude, the Australian Olympic Committee quickly showed its wrath. Actually, the Committee couldn't care less about the full-frontal nudity; it was upset that the calendar identified the players as "Olympic" team members. Under the Sydney 2000 Games Protection Act, it sniffed, the word "Olympic" cannot be used without its permission. The team has agreed to reissue the calendar without the offending word. (AP) ...*Atlanta Olympics: bombs. Sydney Olympics: bombshells.*

Paging Inspector Clouseau: The Canadian Security Intelligence Service is in hot water after a female agent left top-secret files in her car when she went to a Toronto hockey game. They were stolen by drug addicts, who dumped them into the trash, but she didn't report the theft in time for the plans to be recovered — they're now believed to be deep in a trash pile. Worse, the head of the CSIS's oversight board heard about the debacle from the newspaper. And to add insult to injury, agency insiders grumble that female agents aren't disciplined as severely as male agents for such errors. A retired agent told CBC television that "There's no such question as giving someone a break just because he or she is a woman." (Reuters) ...*Which isn't as ironic as you might think, considering the disguises available to agents.*

Notice: Seat Belts Now Required in One-Horse Open Sleighs: Much to the disgust of tradition-minded citizens, state officials in Mississippi declared real Christmas trees a fire hazard. To demonstrate their commitment to safety, the state put an artificial tree on display in the state capitol in Jackson. The artificial tree promptly caught fire, forcing the evacuation of the building. (AP) ...*Now, about those chestnuts roasting in a closed toaster oven....*

Season's Gratings: A poll commissioned by a company that sells gift certificates found that Britons receive 1.6 billion pounds (US$2.6 billion) worth of unwanted Christmas gifts each year. The top unwanted items were home-knitted pullovers, talcum powder, sandwich toasters, and Elvis Presley clocks. Where do the unwanted presents go? Most re-wrap them to pass along to friends. (Reuters) ...*Apparently it really is better to give than receive.*

Scrooge, The Next Generation: Richard Ganulin, an attorney, filed suit against the U.S. government, arguing Congress did not have the authority to declare Christmas a legal holiday because of First Amendment guarantees separating church and state. Cincinnati, Ohio, U.S. District Judge Susan J. Dlott ruled, "We are all better for Santa, the Easter Bunny too, and maybe the Great Pumpkin, to name just a few! An extra day off is hardly high treason; it may be spent as you wish, regardless of reason. One is never jailed, for not having a tree, for not going to church, for not spreading glee! The court will uphold, seemingly contradictory causes, decreeing 'The Establishment' and 'Santa' both worthwhile claus(es)." Ganulin said he will appeal the ruling. (AP) *...The trial court has erred, the lawyer will say. It's illegal to sanction a bank holiday. It's OK for government to say no to a drug, but its position on Christmas must be "Humbug"!*

Naughty, Not Nice

Mexico Church Calls Santa a Drunk

AP headline

Up, Up and Away: Samantha Munns was filling toy balloons in her London, England, toy shop when she fell on the helium tank nozzle. She says she was worried she would explode after it "pumped her full" of helium. "I looked like I was five months pregnant," she said. Doctors dismissed the idea of "popping" her, and decided instead to let her body slowly absorb the gas. "I was thinking that if I died they would have to put me in a giant coffin and people wouldn't know whether to laugh or cry," she said. (Reuters) *...At least her pallbearers would have had an easy go of it.*

In That Case, You're Fired: U.S. presidential candidate Sen. Bill Bradley has blasted companies which don't provide health insurance for their workers. One of his campaign platforms is, in fact, universal health care. But Bradley's campaign office has admitted that some employees of his presidential campaign were not provided with health insurance. However, Bradley spokeswoman Anita Dunn insisted, "If Bill Bradley's health-care plan was already in effect, all of these people would have their choice of coverage." (AP) *...Thus establishing Bradley's "do what I say, not as I do" credentials necessary for the Oval Office.*

Casting Call: Percy has been fired. The 17-month-old Amazon parrot, being used in the play *Pirates on Treasure Island* in Blandford Forum, England, was supposed to sit on Long John Silver's shoulder. During rehearsals, everything went well, with the bird saying "pieces of eight" on cue. But during the live performance, Percy instead shouted out "piss off, mate!" when cued. "I could not believe what I was hearing," said Mark Hyde, who plays Long John Silver. Before anyone could react to the muffed line, Percy added, "bugger off." Hyde said "we all stood there in stunned silence before we burst out laughing." (Reuters) ...*See, that's just the kind of positive feedback that encourages him.*

Fangs for the Memories: Anita Finch, 33, a volunteer at the Los Angeles Zoo, was found dead in her southern California home after being bitten by one of her 10 poisonous pet snakes. Charlene McMorris, manager of the mobile home park where Finch lived, says she knew that at least some of the snakes Finch kept were illegal, but she decided against turning her in to authorities. "That would have killed her," she reasoned. (AP) ...*Either way, she was doomed.*

Millennium Dumb: How can one show just how big a milestone the millennium is? Britain's Millennium Dome in London plans a special film showing human fertilization. Accompanied by a drumbeat by a Senegalese musician who has 38 children, computer-generated sperm will be projected on a screen doing a war dance as they approach an egg, the drumbeat getting more and more rapid to signify a pounding heartbeat. The actual moment of fertilization will be signaled by "the twang of an arrow striking its target." The 45-second film will be shown continuously in the Dome's Body Zone. "What we didn't want to do was to do some terrible boring biology lesson, where sperm run around like headless chickens," said Body Zone spokesman John Hackney. "This is more like a 'Tom and Jerry' film." (Reuters) ...*No, more like a Woody Allen film.*

Adam, Meet Eve: Cable channel MTV has recruited three men and three women to stay in a "millennium bunker" over New Year's eve just in case the world ends. Post-apocalypse, the "bunkernauts" would then presumably emerge to repopulate the world. Bunkernaut Maureen Kyle, 19, of Westlake, Ohio, chosen for "her wholesome midwestern values," says she's prepared for the worst, and that her parents know that her assignment "could entail sex with strangers should civilization reach its end." (AP) ...*But that's OK, since there would be no one around to talk about it.*

Y2K Complacent: Nuclear plants in the Czech Republic will not be affected by the Y2K bug, insists Josef Capek of the State Center for Nuclear Safety. How does he know? The Soviet-designed Temelin plant won't be online until 2001, he says, and even so, what has been built so far will be shut down on New Year's eve, he says. And the Dukovany plant, the only other nuclear power facility in the country, can't be affected by the bug since it's not computerized, it's run on an analog system. (AP) ...*Same with humans, but they seem particularly affected.*

Y2K Comeuppance: The world will end with Y2K, says "Bobby Bible". Bible, 60, an American who refuses to reveal his real name, describes himself as a Conservative Baptist. He is spending New Year's in Bethlehem to warn Israelis, Palestinians, and anyone else who will listen about the coming of the Lord. "On December 31, He will part the sky and come partially down," he tells passersby in Manger Square. "Dead and living Christians are going to go up to meet Him. It's going to be a catastrophe for you and wonderful for me." And what kind of catastrophe might befall those poor non-Christians? "You will come under the wrath of God. You are going to get a spanking," he shouts. (Reuters) ...*Yeah, you know you're really in trouble when God bends you over His knee.*

Y2K Consolation: Just because the *Mir* space station may soon fall out of orbit and burn up in the Earth's atmosphere is no reason to worry about its computers, says the Russian Space Agency. Spokesman Sergei Gorbunov has issued assurances that the aging station's computers are Y2K compliant. (AP) ...*Sure: the computer thinks it's 1973.*

Unlike Last Time

Unusual Millennium Parties Planned

AP headline

Honest: Norman Hardy Jr., 22, pleaded innocent in court in Brattleboro, Vt., to charges of cocaine possession. Then he filled out a form requesting a public defender to represent him. Occupation? "Selling drugs," he wrote on the form. The judge granted the request for a public defender. (AP) ...*Possession of cocaine: guilty. Possession of brain: not guilty.*

Any Luggage? Rodney Carrington told Customs officers at Miami (Fla.) International Airport he had nothing to declare. But officials noticed "wriggling" and "ominous bulges" in "unusual places" in Carrington's pants, said federal prosecutor Thomas Watts-Fitzgerald. They searched him and found he was hiding 55 4-inch red-footed tortoises in his slacks, which he allegedly brought in from Barbados. Carrington was charged with smuggling and the transportation of endangered species. (AP) ...*Trouser tortoises take trip with taciturn traveler, protrude into authorities' attention, trigger arrest. Trafficker apparently thankful contraband didn't attack privates.*

Big Brother is Watching: Researchers in Britain have announced a new security monitor that "predicts mathematically" whether people are contemplating illegal acts even before they commit them. The system, designed by Steve Maybank of the University of Reading and David Hogg at the University of Leeds, watches for the "different behaviors" of people contemplating "suspicious" activity and alerts security guards. Meanwhile, in the U.S., a new x-ray machine installed in several airports that allows operators to scan people — and look through their clothing — is under fire. U.S. Customs Commissioner Raymond Kelley defended the controversial machine. "People object to being physically touched. In response to that we brought in the scanners," he said. (Reuters, AP) ...*Either way, you're being laid bare.*

What's for Dinner? Swedish inventor Bruce Lambert has received a patent on a new refrigerator. His innovation: the door is a mirror that, when a light is switched on inside the fridge, turns into a clear window so users can see the food inside without opening the door. That saves energy, of course. But Lambert notes that's not the only good part. He says the mirror encourages dieting because people can see their reflections as they approach the door. (Reuters) ...*If he really wants it to be effective, he needs to invent a way for people to see their reflections as they walk away from the door.*

Hooked on Fonicks: An internal auditor has found that teachers and administrators at 32 New York City schools helped students cheat on standardized tests. In some cases, test proctors filled in answer sheets for the students. At P.S. 234, the principal would point out incorrect answers and demand that students "do that one over," said Edward Stancik, who oversees 1,100 schools. With that kind of help, P.S. 234's scores for third graders, which measure what percentage of students read at the appropriate grade level, dramatically rose from 29 percent to 51 percent. (AP) ...*In other words, the principal only knows about half of the third-grade vocabulary lessons.*

Equal Opportunity: When the obviously-blind man came into a bank in Memphis, Tenn., the bank's security guard offered to help him to the teller window. The man accepted. Then the man slipped a note to the teller. The surprised teller read it, then mouthed to the guard the words, "It's a robbery!" Bruce Edward Hall, 48, who was not carrying a gun, was easily apprehended by the guard and held for police. He has been charged with robbery. (AP) ...*Social workers need to remember that when they tell their clients "You can do anything," they need to add "with some minor exceptions."*

Log In, Drop Out: Mitch Maddox, 26, says he wants to show people "how to utilize e-commerce." To do that, he legally changed his name to DotComGuy and, on January 1, moved into a completely empty house in Dallas, Texas, taking only a laptop computer with him and promising not to come out for a year. He will have to order everything he needs via the Internet. "We certainly don't recommend that people lock themselves away from the world, but we will prove that it can be done," said DCG's friend Len Critcher, who is helping with the project. After locking himself in, DotComGuy predicted "I'm going to come out being a loon." (AP) ...*As if he had to do a year-long PR stunt to prove that.*

Guess Who's Coming to Dinner? President Clinton invited 350 "American Innovators" to the White House to celebrate the new year. As they streamed in for a New Year's Eve dinner, reporters asked some of them for their thoughts about the past century. Civil rights leader Rev. Jesse Jackson, for instance, said "I celebrate a historic century of struggling and scars and victories." Entertainer Sid Caesar said "The last 100 years we've gone from horse and buggy to the moon and back." Not all of the "innovators" were as profound. Actress Mary Tyler Moore proclaimed the invention of the century was, "I think the blow dryer," and actor Jack Nicholson could only muster "This is America here. Yeah." (Reuters) ...*Unfortunately, Bill forgot to invite any screenwriters.*

Y2.0000000000000000K: The U.S. Naval Observatory's atomic clock is used as a master clock for government activities. The observatory's web page proudly shows the time, accurate to a tiny fraction of a second. Most of the time. Just after midnight on January 1, 2000, the web page showed the current date as "Jan. 1, 19100". (AP) ...*Hey: we said we dealt with time, not dates.*

Y2.0000000000000001K: Dennis Olson was sure the Y2K computer bug would be a huge problem. He spent $20,000 on supplies ("I even have a medical kit equipped for minor surgery.") and clocked 1,000 hours online doing research. "I studied everything there was to know about the power grid, the just-in-time supply system, fuel shipments, food storage, communications and martial law," he said. After seeing the new year come in with barely a hitch, Olson said he was a bit disappointed. "It's a little bittersweet to see it end this way," he said. (AP) ...*Well, there's always next millennium.* *

A Bit Overdone
Chef Gets Life for Cooking Wife
Reuters headline

Don't Ask: The Democratic National Committee, in an admittedly completely unscientific poll, asked its web site visitors what course of action the next president should follow. It was "unscientific" because respondents were self-selected, and because the question was extremely leading: readers were asked "what are the most important priorities facing our next president?" and offering the choice of the Democratic plan of "Saving Social Security, strengthening Medicare, and paying down the debt or implementing [Republican presidential aspirant] George W. Bush's $1.7 trillion risky tax scheme that overwhelmingly benefits the

---

* See http://www.thisistrue.com/y2k.html for much more on the milloonnium madness

wealthy?" The latest results showed Bush's tax cuts winning with more than 72 percent of the vote. (Reuters) ...*Democrats are getting more and more wealthy all the time.*

Reality TV: A clash between reporters and other employees of a cable TV station in Taipei, Taiwan, for control of the station was broadcast live. It went on until four were hospitalized with injuries, and some equipment was destroyed, knocking out the channel's transmitter. (AP) ...*On the plus side, the brawl drew the station's best ratings ever.*

TV Land II: The United Paramount Network has ordered the development of several 15-minute TV shows in an attempt to lure in viewers whose attention spans are too short for 30-minute shows. "The network is experimenting with different ways of appealing to its target audience — teen-aged boys and young men — who are notorious 'grazers' with the remote control," says UPN spokesman Paul McGuire. (AP) ...*And how, exactly, did "teen-aged boys and young men" end up with such short attention spans, Mr. McGuire?*

Dumb: Police in Columbia, Tenn., are searching for a man who robbed the First American Bank. "He came running out with a wad of cash, tried to jump into his car and couldn't open the door," a police spokesman said — he had locked his keys in the car. "When last seen, he was running as fast as he could from the scene." Meanwhile, the FBI in Nashville were looking for a robber who successfully held up a bank by pointing a hot dog at a teller. (Reuters) ...*Which is considered a deadly weapon in Tennessee.*

Dumber: Lying is a social skill, says University of Massachusetts psychologist Robert Feldman, who researched the matter. He studied adolescents aged 11 to 16 and found that the more effective they were at lying, the more likely they were popular among peers. How might that help them in real life? "Politicians have known for a very long time that telling people what they want to hear is a very good social tactic," Feldman says. (AP) ...*Then why don't we like them?*

Dumbest: Effas Ondya, 56, of Lusaka, Zambia, sued his wife Dorothy Mapani, 37, to get a court order vacating a $200 bet he made with her. They have been unable to conceive a child, so Ondya bet his wife that it was her fault, and said she could have sex with other men to prove otherwise. If she didn't get pregnant by February 22, 2000, he would win. But when she said she would proceed with the experiment, he had second thoughts and sued. Zambia's High Court ruled against Ondya. "There is clear indication that you have allowed your wife to have sex with other men," ruled judges Sainet Chiutambo and Joseph Mumba "The bet remains a bet." (Reuters) ...*Either way, she wins.*

Beyond Dumb: It was a routine check-in at the Meador Inn in Van Buren, Ark., the desk clerk said. The man registered for a motel room, even looking in his wallet so he could fill out all the information required on the card. Then he followed the clerk into the back room, robbed her, and fled, she said. Police asked to see the registration card. It showed the name Scott Brady and a local address. Police found that Scott Brady was a real name, and lived at that address. They arrested him and charged him with aggravated robbery. (AP) ...*And with that one registration, he gets a room for the night for 3–5 years.*

It Ain't Easy Being Green: Erik Sprague would like to be a reptile. The 27-year-old philosophy student at the State University of New York in Albany has taken a break from school to appear in circus shows, showing off his sharpened teeth, implanted forehead bumps, and green scale facial tattoos. (Reuters) ...*Most people who want to become a reptile just go to law school.*

It Ain't Easy Being a Lawyer: Linda Ross, a family law attorney in Southern California, is listed in the Yellow Pages. Under "Reptiles". Ross says her mother "laughed for 10 minutes" when she heard about the gaffe in the GTE telephone directory, but is "concerned about what the people who don't know me might think" and worries that the listing might confirm "what they already believe about attorneys." (AP) ... *"Might"?*

It Ain't Easy Being a Graduate: Thanks to ever-looser graduation requirements, high school students in the U.S. are finding themselves unprepared for college or work environments. A high school diploma is thus "a ticket to nowhere," argues Janis Somerville, director of the National Association of System Heads, which represents state universities. "Adding insult to injury, we blame the kids." (AP) ...*Who blame the parents, who blame the teachers, who blame the administrators, who blame the politicians, who pledge to work on it if we will kindly reelect them.*

It's the Thought That Counts

Britain Inches Grudgingly Towards Metric System

Reuters headline

Mr. Conductor Accused of Inside Job: Employees of Crossford Country Park near Lanark, Scotland, watched as workmen loaded up their replica of "Thomas the Tank Engine", a locomotive based on the storybook train engine that the park used to haul kids around on rides. After the workmen finished loading the four-tonne engine onto a truck and drove away, the staffers waved goodbye. It was only then they realized that the workmen didn't work at the park, and the 15,000 pound (US$24,570) engine had just been stolen. "I cannot believe the nerve of these people," park manager James Warnock said when notified of the theft. (Reuters) ...*All thieves have nerves of steal.*

What's Your Poison? James Bond does it right, say researchers at the University of Western Ontario in Canada. According to their study, published in the British Medical Journal, martinis are healthier when shaken, not stirred. "Shaken martinis have a superior antioxidant activity than those that are stirred," they say, although "the reason for this is not clear." But the fictional spy's good health can't all be from martinis, they added. "007's profound state of health may be due, at least in part, to compliant bartenders." (Reuters, AP) ...*And all this time, we thought it was the compliant "Bond Girls".*

Mirror, Mirror: London's Madame Tussaud's museum says their wax figures of Sporty, Scary, Posh and Baby Spice — the Spice Girls — makes the British group the first "complete" rock group they have sculpted in wax since the Beatles. Shown her waxy clone, Melanie "Sporty Spice" Chisholm was asked if she wanted to change any of the effigy's attributes. "I'd like bigger bosoms," she said. (Reuters) ...*While most of the public would like her real voice to be exactly like the dummy's.*

This is a Ssssstick Up! A convenience store in Oklahoma City, Okla., was robbed by a man using a snake as a weapon. The robber told the clerk it was a "copperhead rattlesnake," but police said it was actually a python, which is not poisonous. Lyle Burpo, 21, was arrested and charged with robbery. Police recovered the snake from his car. (AP) ...*Dozens of lawyers have offered to represent him free out of "professional courtesy."*

Mayday: Two rescue boats went into action when Denmark's Maritime Sea Rescue Command was told that a freighter was in distress, with one crewman washed overboard, off Bornholm in the Baltic Sea. They found nothing until the calls were traced to a drunk 52-year-old man playing with toy ships in his landlocked bathtub. He faces a fine of 10,000 crowns (US$1,400) after police charged the unidentified man with calling in a false alarm. (Reuters) ...*Responding officers deny charges they made fun of his dinghy.*

Offensive Defense: Blaine E. Gamble, 60, charged with robbing a bank in Herminie, Penn., while dressed as a woman, says he is innocent of robbery by reason of "cultural insanity" caused by "unwarranted exposure, victimization and repetitive confrontation with white racism." The federal prosecutor assigned to the case did not object to the unusual defense ploy. Meanwhile, the lawyer who represents Michael Ian Campbell, 18, of Cape Coral, Fla., says his client is not guilty of threatening via the Internet to "finish" the job started by student gunmen at Columbine High School in Colorado because Campbell suffers from "Internet intoxication". The defense was formulated by Miami lawyer Ellis Rubin, who previously — and unsuccessfully — tried a "television intoxication" defense in a murder trial. (AP, 2) ...*And their convictions will be appealed on grounds of "legal lunacy."*

Border Mentality: The village of East Grinstead in Sussex, England, has declared its independence. Now calling itself the People's Republic of Ashurst Wood Nation State (PRAWNS), visitors need a PRAWNS-issued visa before they're allowed in. The community's leader, "King Prawn", insists the declaration is serious. "It sometimes feels that the County Council is a very, very long way away and they've never been to visit us," he complained. (Reuters) ...*"We'll crush them like the Sussex-Held Rural Interior Municipal Precinct (SHRIMP) they are," sneered the Council Chairman.*

Lesson Plan: Publisher Princeton Review says it will destroy as many as 225,000 copies of a textbook used over the last 12 years to study for standardized school reading tests. The discussion of the word "cardinal" in *Word Smart II* gives the example, "The cardinal rule at our school is simple. No shooting at teachers. If you have to shoot a gun, shoot it at a student or an administrator." The passage was found by a 12-year-old boy's father. (AP)...*Who was apparently the first person to actually read it.*

Adventures in Print II: "My boys came running into my room screaming, 'Oh, Mommy, look at this'," says Michelle Capdeville of Springfield, Mass. "I'm upset." They showed her their "Barney's Sing-Along Songs" book, featuring songs by Barney, the purple dinosaur. One page included an illustration of a topless woman and some foreign text discussing aphrodisiacs. Publisher Publications International Ltd. said the unintended addition was on the paper used by the Chinese printer, which had reused a leftover roll from a previous printing job, and there were only "a few hundred" of the "defective" books in circulation. (AP)...*Better check out those "I lust you, you lust me" lyrics, too.*

Bad Boy!

X Marks the Spot as Dog Finds Buried Owner

Reuters headline

I C: The Turkish Education Ministry has ordered the publishers of a primary school math tutorial magazine to stop using the letters P and K to stand for unknowns in algebra problems. "PKK" is the acronym for the banned rebel group, the Kurdistan Workers Party. The Ministry suggested *Can Mathematics* magazine use the letters E, G, F and H instead. The magazine agreed. (AP)...*Whereas an American magazine would have responded with the letters F and U.*

Even Your Best Friends Won't Tell You: Sure there are a lot of incompetent people around. The problem is, they don't know it, says Dr. David A. Dunning, a psychology professor at New York's Cornell University, in the Journal of Personality and Social Psychology. He says that the reason they don't know is that the skills people need to recognize incompetence are the same skills they need to be competent in the first place. Thus the incompetent often end up "grossly overestimating" their own competency, even when they're making a mess of things. At the same time, very competent people tend to underestimate their abilities. Dunning notes such studies create a unique danger for the researchers. "I began to think that there were probably lots of things that I was bad at and I didn't know it," he said. (New York Times) ...*If you want to know what they are, just ask your wife.*

Professional Promotion: Monica Lewinsky, the White House intern President Clinton had an affair with that led to his impeachment, is now a spokeswoman for the Jenny Craig weight-loss chain. But some franchisees say they don't want to participate in the ad campaign featuring the president's former mistress, calling her a poor role model. David Lahey, owner of several Jenny Craig outlets in Iowa, refuses to run the ads. "I wouldn't be pleased if my daughter came home and said, 'I want to be just like Monica Lewinsky'," he says. (AP) ...*Though it beats having your son come home and say he wants to be just like Bill Clinton.*

Professional Promotion II: Human rights groups in Argentina are demanding the withdrawal of an ad for Hawaiian Tropic suntan lotion which shows a man getting so tan thanks to the lotion that he is dragged off by the KKK. "The tone is humorous," insists Carlos Perez, the director of the agency that created the ad. "The idea is, you're going to get so black that the Ku Klux Klan are going to come after you!" (Reuters) ...*At least Perez is serving as a warning to others.*

Professional Promotion III: "The Jail", a restaurant in Taipei, Taiwan, has become a popular night spot. The theme of the restaurant, which includes waiters in prison uniforms, is that of a jail mess hall. But decorations included photos of starving concentration camp internees and the restroom signs read "Gas Chamber". Jewish groups were understandably upset. "Taiwanese just aren't that aware of this history and aren't as sensitive about it as foreigners are," said manager Stone Cheng, adding that no Taiwanese patrons complained. Foreign customers did — and the restaurant beat a hasty retreat and removed the holocaust photos. (AP) ...*What better way to stimulate appetites than to show your customers pictures of starving people?*

Captive Audience: When officials in British Columbia, Canada, threw a party, they threw it with style. Pizza, snow cones, popcorn, rented palm trees, games and a bubble-blowing machine. A good time was had by all. But Member of Parliament Myron Thompson was incensed. "I hardly think that prison is meant for those kind of functions," he complained — the party was thrown by the staff at Matsqui Institution, a medium security prison, for the 350 prisoners. Assistant Warden Wayne Marston thinks the party "was a positive event," and noted "it was very well received" by the inmates. (Reuters) ...*Well, OK, as long as they didn't have any open bars.*

Boo! Boo Hoo: The Universal Studios amusement park in Orlando, Fla., opens a Halloween Horror Nights haunted house each year. But Cleanthi Peters, 57, who visited the park in 1998, is suing because the haunted house was too scary. The suit contends that she was so afraid when chased by a costumed employee wielding a chain saw that she fell down, causing unspecified physical injuries and "extreme fear, emotional distress and mental anguish." She demands $15,000 in compensation. (AP) ...*If she thinks that's scary, wait until the attorney chases her down wielding his bill.*

Remember Me: Howard Potter, 51, a spokesman for the Association of Chartered Certified Accountants in Cardiff, Wales, doesn't really remember what he did New Year's eve, but whatever friends are still talking to him have told him plenty. So much so that he was moved to take out an advertisement in the newspaper to offer a "contrite, abject and public apology" to the people he "castigated, vilified, embarrassed or, worst, bored." Then he got his credit card bill. "I couldn't believe it. I could have bought a car with what I spent" that night, he said. Embarrassing enough, but his employer refuses to accept the apology and forced him to resign. "We don't object to him having a drink, but to how he drew it to public attention," sniffed the apparently new spokesman for the ACCA. (Reuters) ...*The headline: "Accounting Body Says Alcoholic Accountants OK as Long as Problem is Kept Hidden".*

Which Came First? A magazine in China dedicated to unidentified flying objects is getting popular, with 400,000 subscribers. And, suddenly, there has been a rash of UFO sightings around the country, with perhaps 500 flying saucers being spotted in 1999, says the China UFO Research Resource Center. But in China, there's little talk of alien abductions for weird medical experiments, as is often heard in the U.S. Rather, says Shen Shituan, the president of the UFO Research Association, the aliens are interested in tourism and investing. "It's very possible that relatively rapid development attracts investigations by flying saucers, and here in China we're becoming more developed," he said. (AP) *...Yes, Mr. Shituan, there are in fact aliens interested in tourism and investing in China. They're called Americans.*

Impressionistic: The two-million-pound (US$3.29 million) Cezanne painting *Auvers-sur-Oise* was recently stolen from England's Oxford University. So when police heard it was hanging in a pub in Coventry, they swooped in to recover it. Publican Nigel Ashby of the Malt Shovel pub said the cops were quite interested. "At first I led them on, waffling about bold use of color and brush style," he said. But the officers didn't believe him. "What gave it away was that the paint was still wet." (Reuters) *...Let me guess, Nigel: you called that tip in yourself, didn't you?*

Not Safe Enough

Police Work a Lot Safer Than in 1970

AP headline

Two Cops Killed Attempting Arrest

AP headline later the same day

I Had a Dream: Virginia used to celebrate Lee-Jackson Day, honoring Robert E. Lee and Stonewall Jackson. But when Martin Luther King Jr's birthday became a federal holiday, the state changed their holiday to Lee-Jackson-King Day. Gov. Jim Gilmore now says honoring all three men on the same day is "confusing" and wants to split them up. "The time has come to enhance these holidays and give them their due recognition," he said. Former Gov. L. Douglas Wilder, the state's first black governor, agrees. "It should be separate. I endorse it wholeheartedly. I think it's great." (AP) ... *Terrific: we've come full circle back to "separate but equal".*

We're Not Glad to See You: Mississippi State Sen. Tom King has introduced an amendment to the state's anti-nudity law to prohibit men from being aroused in public. The new law would prohibit "the showing of covered male genitals in a discernibly turgid state" in any public place. Violations could result in a year in prison and a $2,000 fine. (Reuters) ...*If men had full control over "turgidity", there wouldn't be a market for Viagra.*

On Second Thought: When Greg Pruitt, 23, was out hunting in Florida's Ocala National Forest, he found a World War II-era bomb, probably lost by a nearby naval range. He decided he wanted it "as a keepsake" and hauled it back to camp in his pickup truck. When other hunters saw the bomb, police were summoned and 50 people were evacuated while the military retrieved it. "Looking back," Pruitt said afterward, "common sense should have kicked in a little better." (AP) ...*Just the kind of thing people like to hear from a guy carrying a high-powered rifle.*

Stuart Little on a Binge: Debra Welsh had a problem with mice in her house near Albuquerque, N.M., and she got good at catching them. Especially the "wobbly" ones. "Those little drunken, wobbly mice would get into the house and you could get right up to them and pick them up by their tails," she remembers. "And they would die real fast." After catching the last one, she was hospitalized — with bubonic plague. She's now recovering, and has learned her lesson: no more trying to catch mice on her own. Especially the "wobbly" bubonic carriers. (AP) ...*Sounds like a job for Greg Pruitt.*

Zorro, The Next Generation: Dr. Allan Zarkin, an obstetrician at Beth Israel Medical Center in New York, N.Y., said he did "a beautiful job" on a Caesarean section in the hospital. So he used his scalpel to "initial" his work, carving "AZ" on Linda Gedz's abdomen as she lay sedated on the table, Gedz says in a lawsuit. She is suing Zarkin and the hospital for $5.5 million, saying the three-inch-high letters make her feel "like a branded animal". (Reuters) ... *"While I continue to keep this Oath unviolated, may it be granted to me to enjoy life and the practice of the art, respected* *by all men, in all times! But should I trespass and violate, may the reverse be my lot!" —From the Hippocratic Oath*

Buff: Some body builders don't just pump iron for fun, looks, or health benefits, says Dr. Eric Hollander of New York's Mount Sinai School of Medicine. They are suffering from mental illness: a type of body dysmorphic disorder he calls "bigorexia, which is sort of the opposite of anorexia." Men who suffer the condition think they are too small, no matter how much they work out. The good news, Hollander says, is that such men can be helped with the same drug that treats other obsessive-compulsive disorders. (AP) ...*Don't all men think they're too small?*

Stuff: Ashrita "Mr. Versatility" Furman says he plans to try to get his "world record" certified by the Guinness Book of World Records after riding his pogo stick for a mile in Antarctica. Furman holds the Guinness world record for holding the largest number of Guinness world records, such as yodeling for 27 hours and balancing 57 drinking glasses on his chin. "Breaking Guinness records brings me ever closer to my inner truth," says Furman, a New Yorker. "This is proof that human beings have unlimited potential." (Reuters) ...*More accurately, it's proof some humans waste their potential.*

Bluff: Christopher Michael Camp showed up at Hutchinson Beach Elementary School in Panama City, Fla., claiming he was a pitcher for the Florida Marlins baseball team and offering to talk to the kids. School officials eagerly accepted. The kids weren't as gullible: they found he was unable to answer their questions about the team. That's when principal Joel Armstrong got on the Internet and looked up the team's roster. Camp's name wasn't on it. Police warned him away from the school, but didn't charge him with any crime. Why wasn't Armstrong suspicious of Camp's story? "He seemed a little dense, but you know, that's not unusual with some ballplayers," he said. (AP) ...*Or some school officials.*

The Proof is in the Pudding: Last year, David Phillips got excited when he saw a promotion by the Healthy Choice prepared food company: mail in 10 proofs of purchase and get 1,000 frequent flier miles. Getting 1,000 miles for ten $2 dinners wasn't bad, he figured, but getting them for ten 25-cent pudding cups was better. "I quickly realized that for 25 cents I was getting 100 free miles," the Davis, Calif., man said, so he bought $3,140 worth of diet pudding cups, earning 1.25 million miles, or about $25,000 worth of flights. As if that wasn't good enough, he also donated the pudding to food banks for a tax deduction. (Sacramento Bee) *...The new American Dream: beating the system and laughing all the way to First Class.*

When the Saints Come Marching In: The Virgin Mary and some various saints own a lot of the real estate around New Brunswick, N.J., according to Middlesex County property records. Virgin Mary is on record as having sold 248 properties from 1946 to 1972, and "Saints" sold 1,650. Curious officials figured out the problem. "Some of the names in the records were very long, and truncated to a second line in the computer file," explained County Clerk Elaine Flynn. So the "New Brunswick Greek Catholic Church of the Birth of Saint Virgin Mary" was chopped down to the last two words, and the "New Jersey State of the Church of Jesus Christ of Latter Day Saints" ended up with only the last word, during a computer file transfer to a new system. (AP) *...That's nothing: all the tax bills came from "Sex County".*

Nope: You Also Get to Go By a Really Cool Name

Limp Bizkit Singer: Money's Not All

AP headline

You Can't Tell a Book by its Cover: Isaac Kahan says that when he saw the book *McNally's Dilemma* in the store, he assumed it was written by Lawrence Sanders, since Sanders' name was on the cover. The copyright page, however, reveals the mystery novel was not written by Sanders, but by a ghostwriter, since Sanders died in 1998. When Kahan found out he was "misled," he filed a lawsuit in New York against the publisher claiming unspecified damages. (AP) *...Surely a mystery reader should know to look for subtle clues.*

Penalty Box: Tim "Fish-head" McCrory, a "longtime fan" of the Anchorage Aces hockey team, has sued team owner Michael Cusack over the Alaska team's losing season. The suit says that the Ace's bottom-of-the-standings 11-25-5 record is a result of

Cusack's failure to "properly equip and support players." McCrory claims breach of contract and seeks $2,500 for his two season tickets plus punitive damages. McCrory is known as "Fish-head" since he commonly throws a dead salmon on the ice when the Aces score. (Reuters) ... *Your task: determine who's the biggest loser.*

Keep on Truckin': "The driver told our folks that he saw the light but he didn't know what it meant, so he just kept going," says a spokesman for the Port Authority of New York and New Jersey. The driver, trainee Charles Edward Conyers of Paragould, Ark., was at the wheel of a truck. "His instructor was asleep in the cab at the time," the Port spokesman says. Conyers didn't know what it meant when a stop light flashed at him. The light meant the truck he was driving was too tall to get through the Holland Tunnel. It took an hour to pry it out of the tunnel's mouth. Conyers was charged with careless driving, running a red light and driving a vehicle that is above the regulation height. The instructor was neither identified nor charged. (New York Times) ... *But he presumably will be sued.*

I See Great Transfer of Wealth: The New York City Human Resources Administration has abruptly terminated a program to provide welfare recipients training as psychics to get them off the dole. The Psychic Network, which charges telephone callers $4.99 per minute to speak with psychics, pays "workfare" recipients $10 an hour after taking training offered through the city agency. The only qualifications necessary: a high school diploma and the ability to read, write and speak English. At least 15 welfare clients passed a class in tarot card reading and had been hired by the company. The program was canceled, however, hours after a *New York Times* article alerted the public to the training sessions. (AP) ... *It wasn't completely bogus: even the bureaucrats could sense the public ridicule in advance.*

Moscow, We've Got a Problem: Russia's aging *Mir* space station may not be scrapped after all, officials say. Walt Anderson, an American venture capitalist, has put up $7 million, with promises of $14 million more, to lease the 14-year-old station and renovate it as a high-priced vacation resort. "This is an extremely serious effort," promises Mir Corp. President Jeffrey Manber. "We believe that if we are successful, the renovation of *Mir* will be one of the great undertakings of the century." (Reuters) *...Fourteen years of astronomical and life-science research: boring details. Dumping the equipment to make room for socialite sleep-overs: one of the great undertakings of the century.*

The Decline and Fall of the American Empire — One Item in a Long Series: With ABC currently winning the ratings wars thanks to *Who Wants to Be a Millionaire?*, other networks are trying to figure out how to compete. The United Paramount Network is shooting back with *I Dare You*, which it promotes as "the most dangerous new show of the millennium." Network executives say that if someone is killed on camera, the death won't be aired. But injuries are a different matter. "Everything will be taken on a case-by-case basis," says series creator Bruce Nash. "It depends on what 'seriously injured' means. I think good taste and propriety will prevail." (AP) *...Just like it always does on TV.*

Do It Yourself: "This is something 60 to 70 percent of the public supports. It's not something crazy," says Derek Humphry, 69, the author of *Final Exit*, a suicide how-to book. "There is undoubtedly a hunger for this type of information." Humphrey's manual has sold more than a million copies in 12 languages, but to help spread the concept further, he has made a video version of the book. Some are upset that a Eugene, Ore., public-access cable TV station has agreed to air the video. "I think it's reckless," says a spokeswoman for the Portland-based Compassion in Dying Federation. (AP) *...And it sure can't be good for the station's long-term ratings.*

Take a Bite out of Crime: A police officer in Brisbane, Australia, is recovering after a ferret bit him on the penis. The animal had been confiscated after its owner was cited for keeping prohibited wildlife without a permit, and was being driven to a wildlife refuge. "The ferret got itself out of the box and latched itself to a place of undesirable intent on the police officer's person in the front seat," said a police spokesman. "It caused him a certain amount of reaction and he is getting a lot of sympathy." The officer nearly crashed his car, and had to subdue the critter with his baton. The ferret is in good condition at the refuge. (Australian AP) *...You can't escape the short arm of the law.*

Dinah Blow Your Horn: More and more housing tracts are being built near railroads, and local authorities are trying to get the trains to be more quiet. "We've been working so hard to rebuild and revitalize downtown, and now they say they're going to blow whistles?" gripes Arlington Heights, Ill., Mayor Arlene Mulder. Absolutely, says Federal Railroad Administration Administrator Jolene Molitoris — it's necessary for trains to blow their horns near crossings to reduce the hundreds of deaths each year from collisions. "It is really about life and death and how we can prevent truly preventable injuries and deaths," Molitoris said. No, counters Mulder, "The real threat is to quality of life." (AP) ...*Life can't be any too good when you aren't alive.*

Conclusion: We Must Cause Even More Accidents

Airline Travel Safer Despite More Accidents —Report
Reuters headline

That's It, No Tip: When Amanda Gustafson, 4, was served apple juice at a TGI Friday's restaurant in Marlboro, Mass., she took one sip and said it "tastes yucky, daddy." Her father checked it out and found the cup contained whiskey. "It was a very unfortunate mistake," said the chain's spokeswoman, Amy Freshwater, claiming a waitress picked up the cup and assumed it was the correct beverage. But Amanda's father Ron doesn't buy it. "They blamed it on the waitress, but what is whiskey doing in a plastic cup with a straw?" (AP) ...*Ron's next stop: TGI Lawyers.*

Maritime Moments: The lifeboat station at the Brighton Marina in England was the scene of an ugly theft. First, the keys to the station were stolen, leaving the crew locked out until they could find a spare key. "Who'd break into a lifeboat station? We wouldn't have been able to access our boat," said a spokesman. Worse, "they took our tea and biscuit fund collection." Is that all? Hardly: "They've stolen our whisky, which is the worst thing." (Reuters) ...*Of course, they told their boss it was apple juice.*

The Next Best Thing to Pleading Guilty: Douglas Holmes was out on bail during his Jackson County, Missouri, trial for robbery. As a repeat offender, Holmes faces life in prison, and when he saw the load of evidence and witnesses against him was fairly overwhelming, police say, he grabbed the recovered money being used as evidence and ran out of the courtroom. The judge ordered Holmes arrested, and the trial continued without him. He was convicted of three counts of robbery and three counts of armed criminal action. "I can't believe I lost my money twice," said a victim who was in court to testify against Holmes. (Kansas City Star) ... *That's pretty much the same feeling you get when you pay taxes.*

Three More and He's an Ace: U.S. Air Force security officer Airman Raymone Sydnor, on patrol at Eglin Air Force Base in Florida, dropped his personal cell phone on the floor of his car. As he was groping for it, he managed to drive into a parked F-15 fighter jet. The patrol car was destroyed, the jet suffered $62,000 in damage, and Sydnor received a concussion. Sydnor's punishment was not released, but the base has issued new guidelines for security officers, requiring they get out of their cars for 10 minutes every half-hour "to combat boredom and oxygenate blood flow." (AP) ... *What about a policy of watching where the heck they're going?*

Don't Throw Stones: A government-funded art project in Santiago, Chile, is under attack by a local lawyer who has filed a lawsuit calling it unconstitutional. The project, a glass house where passersby can watch student and actress Daniella Tobar, 21, live her life — including dressing, using the toilet and showering — is "immoral", charges attorney Rene Trincado. He says a "vaguely worded part of the Constitution" prohibits "immoral and bad conduct." A judge has agreed to hear the case. (Reuters) ... *The project may or may not be immoral, but the lawsuit will ensure it's immortal.*

Ratings Expected to Improve: A television executive in Hamar, Norway, has resigned his job. That's normally not newsworthy, but the reason he gave has made him a local hero. His handwritten resignation reads, "I, Leslie Goldsack, am resigning from my job as manager and editor-in-chief for TV-Innlandet so I can have more time to lust after my wife." Goldsack, 44, who had worked at the station four years, has been married to his wife Solfrid, 40, for 15 years. "We never saw each other," he complained. His boss said he accepted Goldsack's resignation "even though I have never seen his wife." (AP) ... *And he wouldn't admit it if he had.*

If You Can't Read This, Thank the Government: The U.K.'s Department of Education has ordered the destruction of 48,000 posters sent to schools across Britain to promote literacy. It urged students to increase their "vocabluary" and learn about writing "though" their own work. Teachers brought the errors to the attention of the government agency. "We are pleased that the teachers are obviously reading the posters," an Education spokeswoman responded. (Reuters) ... *You'd think it would be more difficult than that for someone on the dull side to see the bright side.*

Royal Dunk: The U.S. Coast Guard has rescued Erick Angel. The 20-year-old from Phoenix, Ariz., was aboard the Royal Caribbean cruise ship *Nordic Empress* 12 miles off St. Thomas, Virgin Islands. Crew members said they had seen a man in a restricted area around 3:00 a.m., and when they went to investigate could not find anyone. The crew woke up everyone aboard to do a head count and came up one short. The Coast Guard was called, and Angel was found treading water two hours later. "They told me it was like he was swimming for his life," said USCG spokesman Lt. Johnny Gonzalez. (AP) ... *You're new on the job, aren't you, Gonzalez?*

Took a Bath: The City of San Rafael, Calif., had a great idea to raise $104,000 for a public fountain at a downtown plaza: a Millennium-themed show starring Bonnie Raitt, Huey Lewis & The News, and more than 20 other entertainers. For the event to break even, 11,000 people would have had to pay $225-300 for tickets. But only 6,100 did, leaving the city with a loss of nearly $1.2 million. "It's nothing anyone anticipated," said Mayor Al Boro. (San Francisco Chronicle) ... *Taxpayers will still get their fountain, but it will spew red ink instead of water.*

Blood Bath: A police officer in Berlin, Germany, part of an "elite" bodyguard unit, accidentally shot three other members of his team with a machine gun during a training exercise. "It is not yet known what exactly happened," a department spokesman said. The three officers all survived. (Reuters) ... *Sure he needs more practice, but there's no one left who's willing to train him.*

Blood Bath II: Investigating a report of a man threatening people with a gun, police in Bessemer City, N.C., were approached by the suspect's 5-year-old child as they checked his residence. "Daddy makes bombs," the child said, according to officers.

They indeed found bomb-making supplies and arrested Charles Thomas Barber Jr., 33. He was charged with possession of a weapon of mass destruction and contributing to the delinquency of a juvenile. (AP) ...*No matter what, kids are proud of their daddies.*

Dismal Science: Marriage can be looked at as a market, just as any other supply and demand equation, says Prof. Leonard Felli of the U.K.'s London School of Economics. And what drives that market? Divorce and infidelity, he says. "The marriage market is illiquid if there is an inefficient number of divorces," he said. (Reuters) ...*The world's oldest profession figured out that very supply and demand problem centuries ago.*

Recent Discovery from the World of Research

Study: Drinking, Fainting Connected

AP headline

You Mean They Don't Already? Hawaii State Senator Rod Tam has introduced a bill providing 10-minute naps and snacks to state workers each day. "You read so much, your eyes sometimes burn," he said. "You want to rest your eyes, but you don't want people to think you're sleeping on the job." When he was done rolling his own eyes, Sen. Bob Herkes introduced an amendment requiring state employees to work 10 minutes for every four hours of naps. "Think of how refreshed and vigorous state employees would be if allowed to nap for four hours at a time," he told reporters. Tam found the fun-poking disheartening. "No wonder we're a mess and have no direction in the state of Hawaii," he complained. (AP) ...*Hey, Tam: if you're not part of the solution, you're part of the problem.*

Part of the Problem II: To crack down on drug and prostitution problems, the Sacramento, Calif., Police Dept. conducted a sting operation. Among those arrested was Everett "Reggie" Drew, 57, mayor of the neighboring city of Folsom — which is home of the notorious hard-time Folsom State Prison. "He offered cash as well as a small quantity of rock cocaine for the sex act" Drew and the undercover officer agreed upon, a police spokesman said. Drew was booked on five felony and misdemeanor prostitution and drug counts, and was released after posting a $5,000 bond. (AP) ...*The bad news: he faces 10 years if convicted. The good news: he wouldn't have to move very far away.*

Part of the Problem III: The Tegucigalpa residence of Honduran Supreme Court Judge Hernan Silva was broken into by burglars, but an alert neighbor called police. One of the three burglars was shot and wounded by officers, but the other two escaped. Three police officers remained behind to stand guard. The neighbor who had noticed the burglary later called the police again. "The squad that was left watching the house broke in to carry out a second burglary," Judge Silva said. "They took things that the thieves had left behind." Meanwhile, the suspect that was shot escaped from the hospital, where he was under police guard. (Reuters) ...*Bummer how "To Protect And Serve" got mistranslated to "To Pillage And Steal".*

Cross This One Off Your List: The United Nations would like to make something clear: Iraq may have all the pencils it wants. Rumors that the U.N. is restricting the nation from obtaining pencils — a rumor spread by the Iraqi Embassy in Jordan — are false, the U.N. says. The story goes that the U.N., as part of sanctions against Iraq for invading Kuwait, has banned pencil imports because the graphite in them could be converted to military use. A U.N. spokesman says military conversion of pencil graphite was an "extremely unlikely" scenario, and noted that it had recently allowed a shipment of 3.5 million pencils into Iraq. (AP) ...*But not erasers, since the U.N. wants them to reflect on their mistakes.*

Worse, He Realized They Fit Him: During the 1992 fire at Windsor Castle in the U.K., there was a mad dash to save Queen Elizabeth's personal property. It has now been revealed that a member of the Life Guards, the Queen's "elite bodyguard" unit, tried to steal a pair of her panties in the confusion. "Yes, I admit it. I was planning to steal a pair of the Queen's knickers," says Captain Nick Carrell, who is no longer a member of the Guards. "I was helping to clear out her private apartment when I pulled open a chest of drawers. I was amazed to see it was filled with the Queen's underwear and I put out my hand to take a pair. Suddenly I realized she was standing right behind me, watching my every move. I don't know what she thought, but the Queen didn't say a word. It was all very embarrassing." (Reuters) *...She didn't have to say anything. He knows there can be no knighthood for a knickers nicker.*

Thank You for Calling: Tom Mabe *really* hates telemarketers. "When you're self-employed, you jump when the phone rings, hoping it's a client, not a doggone telemarketer," he said. At first, the Louisville, Ky., musician was patient — "I was nice for weeks!" — but when the calls wouldn't let up he started playing gags on the salespeople. "They'd call about a security system and I'd say, 'I'm robbing the place right now, but you might want to try back later'." He told a funeral parlor trying to sell a burial plan he was waiting for a sign from God as to whether he should kill himself, and the funeral call was it. "You're the angel of death, man," he told him. The gag apparently did not perturb the funeral man. "If we can get the paperwork out to you this afternoon, can you hold off [killing yourself] until tomorrow?" was the reply. (AP) *...Telemarketers driving you to suicide? Don't do it! Please go after the telemarketers instead.*

Easy for You to Say: The London, England, recruiting firm Office Angels has conducted a study that reveals that one in five British office workers don't understand the jargon used by co-workers. Such concepts as the "holistic approach" to management problems and going after "low-hanging fruit" leave them confused, they say. "An awful lot of people use these phrases," says Angels CEO Aled Morris, but "they don't actually know what they mean." Their survey found 65 percent of office workers used such jargon — 30 percent saying they did so to "liven up" meetings and 35 percent to "sound more credible" — but 40 percent found it "irritating and distracting". (Reuters) *...In the B2B world, one must think outside the box to get to a new communications paradigm — or risk a sea change toward e-retribution.*

All We Need is Love: The Gimli Early Middle School outside Winnipeg, Manitoba, Canada, has banned students from hugging because, Principal Donna Kormilo says, the hugging situation was "getting out of hand." Instead, she ruled, students who want to show support to each other should instead pat others on the back, shake hands, or give "high fives." Parents Terry and Cindy Lacosse took exception to the no hugs rule and publicly complained. Area residents have rallied their support — against the Lacosses. The couple says other residents are making "menacing comments," the school board superintendent said the couple had done "a disservice to the school and community," and some suggest the family should "move back to where they came from." Mr. Lacosse says the family is indeed considering moving away from the town. (Reuters) ...*Love is only skin deep, but hate goes all the way to the bone.*

Down Under Love for Princess Anne's Daughter
Reuters headline

Who? When you need a shoulder to cry on, whose shoulder do you seek out? If you're British, you probably talk to the man behind the bar, not a clergyman. In a poll, 35 percent said they would talk to a publican, while 10 percent said they'd consult with their vicar and four percent would go to a social worker. "Many people see the pub as a sanctuary, a bolt hole from the hurly-burly of a stressful lifestyle," explained psychologist David Lewis. Or, "perhaps people feel they can reveal their secrets to a pub landlord without being judged. (Reuters) ...*Or, perhaps the refreshments are simply better.*

What? Deo Dubbs, 88, of Sarasota, Fla., has been arrested in a drug sweep, police say. Dubbs admits experimenting with drugs — "I really have nothing else to do. I get lonely and get tired of watching the tube," he says — and was arrested after allegedly buying two rocks of crack cocaine. He even carefully negotiated the price down with the undercover officer, police say. "I'm pretty well thought of at the Senior Friendship Center," Dubbs says, though the arrest may "spoil whatever reputation I have." That's the least of his worries: he faces a $5,000 fine and up to five years in prison if he's convicted. (AP) ...*Buddy, if you think the tube is boring, wait until your cellmate dictates what channel you watch.*

When? Fox TV's rating coup with *Who Wants to Marry a Multimillionaire?* has turned into a fiasco. There are charges that groom Rick Rockwell isn't really a multimillionaire and allegedly abused a former girlfriend. And bride Darva Conger, who met Rockwell on the show, wondered in public "what was I thinking?" and has declared the match over. Fox executive Sandy Grushow now says the network's exploitation shows are done for too. "They're gone; they're over," he said, promising to eliminate "anything that is exploitative, that reeks of desperation, anything that's merely out for ratings." (AP) ...*Which pretty much would eliminate their entire lineup.*

Where? Alexander Loschke, 35, of Sulzbach, Germany, says he has found the cure for the common cold: a pair of copper wires that a sufferer simply inserts ...up his or her nose. He got the idea from his tomato plants after putting copper on their vines stopped them from rotting. He said he tried wires in his nose when his last cold started, and felt better within 36 hours. Loschke's pretty sure shoving wires up your nose is reasonably safe. "I thought what did the tomatoes good can't do me any harm," he said. (Reuters) ...*And sure enough, Loschke will end up being planted deep underground.*

Why? Massachusetts lingerie manufacturer UndercoverWear planned a fun program to donate 20,000 nightgowns plus $200,000 in cash to homeless shelters. They proposed asking customers to send in photos of themselves in their "ugliest nightie". For each photo received, UndercoverWear would donate a new $40 nightgown plus cash to a shelter. But the idea was shelved when the Washington, D.C., based National Coalition for the Homeless would have nothing of it. Executive Director Mary Ann Gleason said the Coalition would not participate in the offer because the company "exploited women" with its "sometimes-naughty products". Worse, the ugly nightgown idea "just felt weird to me," she said. (AP) ...*Mary Ann, would that be more or less "weird" feeling than sleeping in a dumpster?*

How? Presidential hopeful George W. Bush is following in his father's footsteps in more ways than one — by following in his verbal missteps. Appearing at an elementary school in Nashua, N.H., he told students "This is Preservation Month. I appreciate preservation. This is what you do when you run for president. You've got to preserve." The students were actually observing "Perseverance Month". At another campaign stop, he told voters about growing up during the Cold War. "When I was coming up, it was a dangerous world and you knew exactly who 'they' were. It was us versus them and it was clear who them was. Today we are not so sure who the they are, but we know they're there." (Reuters) ... *"The most important question to ask about education is, 'Is your children learning?'" —G.W. Bush*

Huh? A poll of 9- and 10-year-old children in European Union states reveals several misconceptions and holes in their knowledge. When asked where cotton comes from, for instance, three-quarters didn't know. One-quarter of them answered "sheep". The kids also theorized that bananas grow in Britain and the Netherlands produces olive oil. (Reuters) ...*If you really want to be entertained, ask them where babies come from.*

The Day the Clown Cried: Comedian Jerry Lewis, 73, was honored recently for his life work by the U.S. Comedy Arts Festival in Aspen, Colo. He spoke of the various comics he enjoyed, such as Dean Martin, but didn't mention any women. An audience member asked Lewis which female comics he admired. "I don't like any female comedians," he answered. "A woman doing comedy doesn't offend me, but sets me back a bit. I, as a viewer, have trouble with it. I think of her as a producing machine that brings babies in the world." (AP) ...*Apparently,* The Patsy *will soon need to* Fight For Life *or at least protect* The Family Jewels *— unless* The Nutty Professor *argues* The Ladies Man *is finally* Cracking Up *and has gone* Way... Way Out.

Jungle Justice: When Saul Solis, a fifth-grader at Reagan Elementary School in Abilene, Texas, brought up his grades, his mother rewarded him with a "Tarzan" T-shirt. He proudly wore it to school, but Principal Alan Lockett banned the shirt because other students made "inappropriate comments" about the cartoon character wearing a loin cloth. "It's impossible to make a complete list of what you can and cannot wear" at school, said School Superintendent Charles Hundley in backing up the principal. (AP) ...*So who did something wrong, the kid for wearing the shirt, or his classmates who made "inappropriate comments"? Extra credit: who should get punished?*

No, Daddy, Really!
"The Pill" Might
Prevent Acne Too
AP headline

OK, As Long As They're Warm: The city council of Gretna, La., has voted unanimously to make it legal to throw panties from Mardi Gras Carnival floats into the parade audience. Originally, panties were included in an ordinance that made it illegal to throw anything that represented "male or female genitalia, is lewd or lascivious and includes, but is not limited to, condoms and inflatable paraphernalia." But when the spokesman of a local marching club complained that "panties have been a legitimate throw for Mardi Gras for years," the council deleted panties from the no-throw list. "So we're pro-panties — it's on the record," Gretna City Councilman Vincent Cox announced. (AP) ...*After realizing that going on record as a "no panties council" might have sent the wrong message.*

Zydeco No-No: The New Orleans, La., Police wants to remind revelers that an old Mardi Gras Carnival tradition — throwing beads from balconies as a reward to women who bare their breasts — is illegal on two counts. Tossing anything from a balcony is illegal, and has been since 1956, they say, and baring breasts is illegal under indecent exposure laws. The police decided to remind people of the laws after *Playboy* magazine "encouraged illegal behavior" by giving tips on how to get the best photos of flashing women. "There's no huge crackdown on Carnival fun," a police spokesman insisted, but "it would be irresponsible of us not to respond to [the article]. After all, we are the police department." (Reuters) ...*F-stop, flesh-stop, what's the difference?*

Nothing to Hide: As Terry Richards, 28, was leaving the Springfield Mall in Springfield, Va., a security guard confronted him and accused him of shoplifting. Richards denied taking anything, and allegedly pulled down his pants to prove it. As shocked shoppers gaped, the security guard, apparently not distracted by the full frontal display, found a pair of athletic shoes hidden in Richards' jacket. Police arrested him for shoplifting, and added a charge of indecent exposure, too. Police officer Katie Hughes theorized, "I guess he put them in the back of his jacket so, when he dropped everything, nothing was revealed." (AP) ...*A statement Richards will use as a defense against the indecent exposure charge.*

The Naked and the Damned: Harold Gunn, a Texas state representative candidate, says it's no big deal that he produced and starred in the movie *The Great Texas Showoff,* which features multiple scenes of naked women rubbing motor oil on themselves, dancing, or running through city streets. "It was a blast, something I did 20 years ago," Gunn says. "There is no sex and no dirty language. It's as tasteful as it can get with naked women in it," he says — the women "are all pretty." The Republican candidate, trying to unseat the Republican incumbent, says "It's just no big deal, it shows I am a communicator and that's all." (Houston Chronicle) ... *"If only I had thought of saying that," said an admiring Bill Clinton.*

Danger — Flying Toasters: When former President George Bush was supposedly "amazed" to see a bar code scanner in a supermarket, it was held up as an example of how out-of-touch the president was, even though presidents aren't exactly known for grocery shopping trips. Bill Clinton has now outdone the man he replaced. During a visit to a senior citizen's center in Palm Beach Gardens, Fla., his attention was caught by a series of graphics on a computer screen — coffee cups, deer, and a blackboard — as they morphed from image to image. "Amazing!" the president exclaimed. The graphics were part of a "screen saver" program. (Reuters) ...*Of course he was amazed: politicians don't know anything about saving.*

Who Wants to Be a Sidekick? After a 15-year run, Kathie Lee Gifford has announced she is quitting the *Live with Regis & Kathie Lee* show when her contract is up this summer. Co-host Regis Philbin, who also hosts the game show *Who Wants to Be a Millionaire?,* has stood beside Gifford through her various scandals, inane talk about her son, and her husband's public affair. "It's the right time," she says, adding she wants to "spread my creative wings" and do more singing. Philbin's contract for the fourth-rated daytime talk show extends a year beyond Gifford's, and he says he will continue the show without her. (AP) ... *"And* *that is your final answer!" he shouted before she could change her mind.*

And the Band Played On: Just how bad has crime become in Argentina? Just ask Congress: it's been robbed. Three armed men walked right by security police and through a metal detector at the Congress building in Buenos Aires — which didn't go off, since it was broken — and went straight to the lower house's treasury, where workers were preparing to pay 500 employees with US$1.2 million in cash. They grabbed the money and escaped without having to fire a shot. "It does really seem ridiculous that a place like this, which should be guarded, can be held up," admitted National security chief Enrique Mathov. "This was no ordinary band of criminals," said the chairman of the Chamber of Deputies, Rafael Pascual. "They had a lot of information about how Congress works." (Reuters) ...*Whereas in the U.S., Congress is an ordinary band of criminals.*

Incredible: When a substitute teacher at J. Henry Higgins Middle School in Peabody, Mass., told students that "Hitler is cool," many of the seventh-grade students were offended and reported the unidentified teacher to the principal. Principal Jane Wilson and Superintendent Louis Perullo asked him for an explanation. The teacher claimed that what he meant was that Hitler is dead, therefore his body was cold. Neither administrator found the excuse "credible," and the teacher has been banned from ever teaching in the city's schools again. (AP) ...*Any school teacher that can't instantly spot a lame excuse is obviously incompetent in the first place.*

Scoot: No, not pooper scoopers, pooper scooters. That's what Rome, Italy, will be trying to clean up after dogs — a fleet of scooters with poop vacuums and a water sprayer to make the streets more presentable. Five will be mobilized on a trial basis, and if they prove effective, more will hit the streets. (AP) ...*They'll hit the streets for as long as the dogs do.*

Smile: A photographer in Mexico City was on the street snapping photos when a robber stuck a gun in his face and demanded, "Give me everything you've got," the photographer, identified only as J.V., says. "Please, it's my equipment," J.V. replied. That's when the robber reconsidered. "Better yet, take my picture!" J.V. complied, snapping a pose of the smiling robber, his gun evident in the photo. As the robber basked in his glory, J.V. ran. The photo appeared on the front page of the newspaper *Reforma*. (Reuters) ...*And on page 23 of* Reformatory.

Sequestered: Alyson Fuchs was excited when she was summoned for jury duty. The mailed summons threatened a $1,000 fine or jail time if she didn't appear, but the threat was unnecessary — she reported to the Supreme Court in Brooklyn, N.Y., hoping to be assigned to a criminal trial. And she looked forward to the pay a juror gets: $40 per day. "It's more than my allowance," she said. Alyson is 9 years old, and state law requires jurors to be 18. She was sent home with an apology from the court. (AP) ...*No doubt she is now drawing up papers demanding severance pay.*

The Naked and the Demand: Austrian clothing chain Kleider Bauer's three-week-long promotion will end early, it has announced. The retailer promised to give US$385 in free clothing to the first five shoppers to come into each of its 40 stores completely naked each week. "Dozens" of nude shoppers were lining up each morning in near-freezing temperatures waiting for the doors to open, newspapers reported. Despite the success of the promotional gimmick, the chain canceled the scheme after a store manager received a death threat. It noted the approval of the stunt by customers "was not worth exposing workers to personal attacks and murder threats." (Reuters) ...*If the customers are exposed, it's only fair that the clerks should be too.*

Too Well, It Would Seem

Uganda Facing
Condom Shortage

AP headline

Ugandans Enjoying
the Good Life

apparently unrelated AP headline later the same day

Losers Weepers: A couple living outside Dallas, Texas, found a bag containing nearly $300,000 in cash and a 9mm handgun, and turned it over to police. It has not been claimed by anyone, but the police say the couple cannot claim the cash under "finder's keepers" common law. Because the money had traces of cocaine on it, "the [Drug Enforcement Administration has] determined this is drug money," said a spokesman for the Dallas Police Department. "It is not the same thing as finding a wallet." The anonymous couple is fighting back, retaining an attorney who has pointed to studies that show most U.S. currency has traces of cocaine on it. The DEA advises them not to pursue their claim. "It was found in the middle of the highway with a loaded 9mm on top," says DEA spokesman Frank Seib, pointing out that if it is drug money, they'll want it back. "Somebody is coming after it." (AP) ...*Then you better let them keep the 9mm too.*

Stiff Upper Lip: City officials in Dover, England, say Terry Lee cannot fulfill the final wish of his recently deceased wife, Ruth, who wanted to be buried in the garden outside their house. The local council has obtained an injunction against the burial, suggesting he bury her ashes there instead, so Lee is upping the stakes. "My wife was completely against cremation. I intend to have her embalmed, which is 100 percent preserved, and put her in the front room if I have to," he says. That may be a problem too, however, because of the length of the battle. After being stored in the hospital morgue for six weeks, the body may no longer be fit for embalming, a local official says. (Reuters) ...*An extra benefit of being in the living room is she'll be able to see the garden quite a bit better.*

Loop de Loophole: Bob Lemke is in a war with the town of Cleveland, Wis., over a new ordinance limiting adult entertainment. He was about to sue in order to keep his business, Teasers, open, but when researching the ordinance in preparing his suit, he realized he didn't need to sue when he saw the law exempts performing arts centers, civic centers and dinner theaters. "I'm not going to spend money on a lawyer until [the town] makes me," he says. He has renamed his saloon the Teasers Exotic Dancer Dinner Theater. "I'm a dinner theater," Lemke says with an apparently straight face. "I serve pizza." (AP) ...*Not to mention cheesecake.*

Lent Loophole: Catholics have returned to the tradition of meatless Fridays, but this year St. Patrick's Day falls on a Friday, meaning the devout cannot partake in the American St. Pat's tradition of corned beef and cabbage dinners. Thus the Archdiocese of Boston, Mass., has granted a special dispensation, though church officials in some other areas have not been so accommodating. But no worries: if you're a resident of a parish not covered by a dispensation and need your corned beef, you can just pop over to Boston. "The application of a dispensation applies to the geographical region you happen to be in, not to you as a person," confirms David Early, spokesman for the National Conference of Catholic Bishops. (AP) ...*It's kind of like how some people talk of morals while in church, but then do what they want once they get outside.*

She Probably Whistles in the Wind: Heather Perry, 29, decided she had found a cure for her myalgic encephalomyelitis — "which leaves sufferers feeling permanently exhausted" — but doctors near her home in Gloucester, England, refused to implement it. Perry decided that drilling a hole in her head, a headache treatment from the Middle Ages known as trepanation, would do the trick. Faced with doubting British doctors, she flew to the U.S. for a consultation. American doctors wouldn't help either, but gave her some "medical advice," so she performed the procedure on herself in front of a mirror. Despite drilling too deeply and nearly puncturing her brain, "I have no regrets," she said. "I generally feel better and there's definitely more mental clarity." (Reuters) ...*No one doubts you have a problem with mental clarity, dear.*

Rank Remedy: The City of Los Angeles, Calif., reeling over a police corruption scandal, is facing what it expects will be as much as $125 million in liability over falsified evidence in criminal prosecution. Such an amount would be a huge burden on the city's budget, but Mayor Richard Riordan has an idea of how to pay for it: from the city's share of the "national tobacco settlement" — expected to be up to $300 million. The tobacco money was meant to pay for increased health care costs for taking care of smoking-related illnesses, but the scandal "is the best use of these dollars," Riordan says. (AP) ...*Riordan got the idea when lawyers told him the evidence against the city was "as plain as a smoking gun."*

Caveat Pedester: Norman Green, 51, was crossing the street in Leicester, England, and was hit by a bus. Green survived, and sent the bus operator a claim for damages. The bus company responded by sending him a bill for 526 pounds (US$845) for repairs to the bus's front end. "This accident happened because Mr. Green was not looking where he was going," a company spokesman said. (Reuters) ...*That probably won't be the end of this story.*

First Things First: Before emptying the vaults of the bank in Golczewo, Poland, the robbers stopped by the police station, where only one officer was on duty. They tied him up so they could complete the heist without interruption. "It's the first time in my career that I've heard of bandits attacking a police station," a police spokesman said. (Reuters) ...*Since it worked, it probably won't be the last time, either.*

Had to Outdo Gore's "Invention of the Internet"

Clinton Claims Credit
for Y2K Quash

AP headline

The Show Must Go On: Forty Oscar statuettes, being shipped to Hollywood for the Academy Award ceremony, have apparently been stolen, the Academy of Motion Picture Arts and Sciences has announced. Several boxes of the coveted golden men went missing from a Roadway Express shipping dock, but the Academy says they will have enough awards for the upcoming presentations. Earlier, the Academy revealed that 4,000 ballots mailed to voting members were misrouted to a slow bulk mail facility, rather than sent by first class mail. (Reuters) ...*Coming next year: an award for the Best Snafu.*

And the Winner Is: Everyone wants to be a winner. Entertainment awards are growing by leaps and bounds, with 332 ceremonies last year, up 81 in just two years. Not just for best actors, directors, writers and cinematographers, either: there are now awards for the best publicity campaigns, best hair styling, and best raising of social awareness. (AP) ...*Maybe that "Best Snafu" award idea is more likely than I thought.*

Emetic Awards: If you think TV game shows like *Who Wants to Marry a Multimillionaire?* are starting to stretch the bounds of taste, consider *Anything for Money,* a feature on Peru's highly rated *Laura en America* talk show starring Laura Bozzo, a Lima attorney. The feature paid contestants to do what most people wouldn't normally do: $30 for a woman to lick the armpits of a body builder who hadn't bathed in two days, or $20 for three men to eat a bowl full of live Amazon tree grubs — apparently only giving the money to the man who finished them first. (AP) *...It could be worse: in the U.S., people are willing to be humiliated on the Jerry Springer show for free.*

Look Into My Eyes: Police in Cilacap, Java, have arrested a shaman who tricked female patients into having sex with him. Shaman Suryono, 36, allegedly claimed he has magical powers that enable him to grant people's wishes. He required female clients to bathe and lie naked in his house, and then "they were told that while in the room if a man approached them looking like Suryono it was actually a genie who would make their wishes come true as long as they did what this supposed genie said," a police spokesman says. In addition to having his way with at least 35 women, Suryono also got away with charging them high fees. (Jakarta Post) *...A fact he will use as proof of his magical abilities.*

Down the Hatch: If you enjoy your pints of stout, trim your moustache. A study commissioned by Irish brewer Guinness found that getting froth in your facial hair means you're not getting it in your mouth, resulting in "significant Guinness wastage as a result of inter-fibre retention at every sip," the company said in a statement. A trim moustache results in about nine pounds (US$14) in waste per year, while a full beard could cost up to 23 pounds (US$37). (Reuters) *...If you're spilling it all over your face, you've had enough anyway.*

Hail the Chief: President Clinton, hosting the annual Malcolm Baldrige National Quality Awards at a hotel, was on the podium making his remarks when an alarm sounded. Unsure at first what the interruption was, he joked "The Marriott is not a candidate for the Baldrige Award." As it continued, the president finally demanded, "Could somebody tell me what the deal is?" A fire alarm, he was told. "Are we supposed to leave?" Not yet, an aide answered. "Not yet? That's not an encouraging answer," Clinton complained. About that time, the Secret Service swarmed into the room and hustled Clinton and 1,000 guests out — there was indeed a small fire, and the hotel was being evacuated. (AP) ... *The "not yet," then, was apparently because women and children were going first.*

Security Detail II: When on official business, German Chancellor Gerhard Schroeder is chauffeured in a bullet-proof limousine. But per German law, he must pay 686 marks (US$340) per month in taxes for the perk. If he used the state-owned car for personal business, he'd have to pay substantially more in taxes, so instead he drives his wife's Volkswagen. But he's not completely unprotected: when he's on the road in his wife's car, his bodyguards follow right behind — in a bullet-proof limousine. (Reuters) ...*At least they'll be alive to tell the story of how Schroeder was ambushed.*

M-mmm Good: New Jersey-based Campbell Soup Co. is recalling more than 168,000 cans of its Healthy Request Vegetable Beef Condensed Soup after a soft drink can accidentally went through a vegetable dicer preparing the soup's ingredients. The problem was discovered when three cans of soup were found to have pieces of the can inside. (AP) ...*Campbell decided the recall was cheaper than starting a new ad campaign claiming the soup was high in aluminum.*

Ich Bin Ein Action Figure: Toy maker Hasbro has announced they will make a special edition "G.I. Joe" doll bearing the likeness of President John F. Kennedy. He will be wearing his World War II Navy lieutenant's uniform, and packaged with accessories based on his "PT 109" days. Royalties will be paid to the JFK Library Foundation. Next year, it will release a second JFK doll, dressed in Navy dress whites. Hasbro has said it does not plan to make a Jackie Kennedy companion doll. (Reuters) ...*Though, curiously, Mattel simultaneously announced its new "Marilyn Monroe Barbie".*

We Said No Starch, and We Mean It

Feds Step Up
Laundering Crackdown

AP headline

Who's Calling? When a man called for "Kennedy" on his cell phone, Jeff Jackson of the Cayman Islands told the caller he had the wrong number and hung up. The phone rang again. The same man insisted he had the right number, and wanted to buy cocaine. Jackson took the caller's number and said someone would get back to him. Jackson happens to be the deputy chief of the combined Police and Customs Drugs Task Force for the Caymans. He passed the information to an undercover officer, who arrested Canadians Jason Robertson, 26, and Thomas Valliere, 24, for attempting to buy drugs. They were fined $1,000. (Reuters) *...Finally: authorities who take the wrong number problem seriously.*

Who's Counting? Students in Florida are allowed to use calculators when taking the state's Comprehensive Assessment Test. In fact, the state provides the only calculators allowed for use during the test. But the state is investigating because the Casio calculators they supplied to more than 17,000 students sometimes gave the wrong answers, such as 3 times 3 times 3 equals 81. (AP) *...At least now we know what happened to all those defective Pentium chips.*

Deathwish: Police were confronting a kidnap suspect when he dropped into a crouch and pointed something at them. Rocklin, Calif., officers thought it was a gun and fired. After being shot, Kenneth Lawrence Robertson, 36, told officers, "Thank you, thank you. I'm a bad person. Thanks for shooting me." But it was not a gun he had pointed, it was a cell phone. On the way to the hospital, Robertson asked paramedics to convey his apology to the officers for his attempting "suicide by cop" — faking the officers into thinking he had a gun so they would shoot him. Robertson didn't die, but the officers involved are upset at the ploy. "Who rationally pulls a cell phone on four armed police officers?" a spokesman complained. (Sacramento Bee) *...Want to know something even more stupid? Some cops think felons act rationally.*

Let's Fly: Police in Colorado know they don't like it, but they're not sure what to do to stop it. Skiers and snowboarders have found the ideal terrain near a highway in Silverplume that allows them to jump over cars on the highway. Drivers are startled to see skiers sailing 40 feet above them, jumping the 60-foot gap in the snow cut by the road. Several of the daredevils have been injured when they didn't make it, but no one has been killed. "The sheriff says we could charge them for not having a pilot's license," joked a sheriff's spokesman. But "I don't know exactly what we'd [really] charge them with — other than stupidity." (AP) ...*Isn't that really what, in the end, most people in prison are guilty of?*

War Games: The tension between India and Pakistan has increased again, now that India's Border Security Force captured yet another hawk. The bird caught the BSF's attention since it was "fitted with [an] antenna and a live transmitter flying across the international border," the agency reported. (Reuters) ... *With luck, they'll soon be catching doves instead.*

Blackout: When the cops stopped by Suzanne Meyers' Roseville, Mich., home with an arrest warrant, she was at a loss: she didn't remember being cited for alcohol possession — 14 years ago. "I've been wracking my brain. I don't even remember this," she said. "A warrant's a warrant," shrugged a police spokesman. "The officer had no way of knowing it happened when she was 16 years old." A judge threw out the ancient charge, but Meyers still has no idea what it was about. "I have never even had a speeding ticket." (AP) ... *Yeah, like we're going to trust your memory on that.*

Shooting Pain: Tirisa Ruiz, 43, attempting to smuggle a gun into Picota prison in Bogota, Colombia, thought she could get it past security if she shoved it deep into her rectum. "Deep" is relative: she had to undergo emergency surgery to remove it from her colon. Meanwhile, authorities at the Bogota airport were suspicious of a woman trying to board a flight when her passport photo showing short hair didn't match her towering locks. A search found a packet of more than a pound of cocaine glued to her head, under a wig. "It was glued in there so strongly that efforts to remove it by hand were ineffective," state police said. (Reuters, AP) ...*So the poor cops had to resort to removing it by nose.*

Midnight Express: Alison Mary McKinnon, 37, of Great Britain was passing through security at the airport in Istanbul, Turkey, when the metal detector went off. A search revealed 3 kilos of heroin strapped to her chest. Heroin doesn't set off metal detectors; a more detailed search found that an "intimate body piercing" had done it. Officials refused to specify exactly what was pierced, but did say she faces up to 30 years in prison for drug smuggling. (Reuters) *...You tell kids how dangerous piercings are, but they just don't listen.*

Stick With Us: The director of a Hudson, Mass., day care center has been fired for a stunt the director thought was "funny." A state investigation found several cases of possible child abuse, but none more perplexing than the unnamed director using duct tape — which "works on everything" — to stick a baby to the wall. "Although the motive for such conduct is not clear at this time," investigators said, "at least one staff member stated that the director and the staff would get 'a kick out of doing that'." Two of the staff were also fired. (AP) *...As well they should, for not knowing Velcro is much more appropriate for wall mounting.*

Go Home!
Y2K Crisis Center: What To Do?
AP headline

A Little Off the Bottom: Police in Laval, Quebec, Canada, heard the rumors and conducted a two-month-long undercover operation to see if they were true. A salon in town, Le Salon Sex Symbol, reportedly offered extras with haircuts: depending on how much customers paid, police say, hair stylists would talk dirty, show their breasts, strip naked, or even engage in sex. Three female stylists and five male customers were arrested, charged with working in or frequenting a house of prostitution. And haircuts? "We found some hair on the ground," a police spokesman confirmed. "One of the men got his hair cut. They have a few clients who just go for that." (AP) *...Perverts.*

And the Oscar for the Best Undressed Goes To: The recent Academy Awards allowed a number of movie experts to show their specialized knowledge. None more than Mr. Skin, an expert on movie nudity. He was in special demand for the 2000 awards since all 10 of the nominees for best actress and best supporting actress have, at some point in their careers, done nude scenes. Mr. Skin, 37, who won't reveal his real name, has video clips of them all in the all-together — as well as 1,100 other actresses, in a massive collection he started when he was 17. A strange hobby?

"Some guys collect baseball cards," Mr. Skin says. "I do this." (Reuters) ...*While other guys try to think about baseball when perusing the collection.*

Birds II: Wildlife officials in Bowie, Md., are perplexed as to why birds are falling dead. About 200 starlings fell from the sky along Route 50, some hitting cars on the highway. Several of the bodies were taken for necropsies to determine the cause of death. Steve Noyes, a bird expert at the U.S. Fish and Wildlife Service's National Wildlife Center in Laurel, Md., didn't sound overly concerned about the problem. "It's just a great mystery," he said, but "it's not like it's a great loss." (Washington Post) ...*Starlets, starlings — they never get any respect.*

Got Sarcasm? Mothers Against Drunk Driving is mad. The advocacy group has demanded that People for the Ethical Treatment of Animals withdraw an ad campaign urging people not to drink milk, parodying a dairy ad with the slogan, "Got Beer?" A MADD spokeswoman complained they were "appalled" with the ad "for the simple fact that underage drinking is the number one drug problem among American youths." But a PETA spokesman countered, "College students are savvy. Nobody's going to put beer on their Cheerios ... as a result of our campaign." (AP) ...*Right: they already do that anyway.*

Rules are Rules: Law enforcement officials in Baltimore County, Md., really wanted to capture Joseph Palczynski, wanted for kidnaping and multiple murders. A $10,000 reward was put on his head. Shortly afterward, Andy McCord called 911 for help since Palczynski was smashing his way into his apartment. He held McCord, his girlfriend, and their 12-year-old son hostage. After a lengthy siege, they were able to escape, and McCord has asked for the reward. But Metro Crime Stoppers won't give it to him. "He did not convey the information according to Metro Crime Stoppers rules" because he called 911, not the Crime Stoppers "tip line", a spokesman said. "And [his call] did not lead to the arrest of Mr. Palczynski," he continued — because police did not arrest him. They shot him to death when they stormed McCord's apartment. (AP) ...*You've always got to read the fine print.*

Rules II: Customers getting their hair done at The Clipping Company salon in Renton, Wash., were startled by an upset young woman who burst into the shop to ask to use the telephone. The woman had parked in a marked handicapped-only space, even though she is not disabled, and another motorist allegedly damaged her car in anger over her taking the spot. The woman wanted to report the other motorist to the police. "It's nobody's business where I park!" she told patrons at the salon. When police arrived, they took quick action: they gave the woman a ticket for parking in a handicapped spot without a permit. (Seattle Times) ...*Then again, lots of people don't read the bold print, either.*

Social Studies: Two middle school students were quickly arrested in Chimacum, Wash., after police learned they were conspiring to shoot several classmates, teachers and school administrators. The two, a boy who came up with a plan and a girl who helped refine it by allegedly suggesting they cut phone lines so the victims couldn't call for help, were charged with conspiracy to commit first-degree murder. Attorney Craddock Verser said he would call for the charges to be dismissed. "She's a 14-year-old kid. He's 12. They're not going to kill anybody," he argued. (AP) ...*Right: only 6-year-olds kill classmates.*

Evidentiary Procedure: Police in Hollywood, Calif., were chasing a car driving erratically late at night. Allegedly the driver, Sam Otero, 30, wanted to get rid of some evidence before he pulled over. "When the suspect tried to throw a beer can out of the car, he opened the door and fell out onto the street," a police spokesman said. Otero was quickly captured, taken to a hospital for treatment of minor injuries, and booked on suspicion of driving under the influence of alcohol. (Reuters) ...*And, presumably, failure to wear his seatbelt.*

Now That We're Really, *Really* Sure She's Not Coming Back
Titanic Shipyard
May Sack Workers
AP headline

Foresight: Billionaire software developer Michael Saylor of Virginia is donating $100 million to establish a free Internet-based university. And if that's not enough money to accomplish the goal, "I'll contribute more over time until it's done," he said.

There are other online schools, but Saylor wants his to be free for anyone. "Done right, this will impact the lives of millions of people forever," he said. "Done wrong, it's just noise in a can." (AP) *...Just like the Internet in general.*

Annoy Jane: In 1997, billionaire Ted Turner stunned the world by donating $1 billion to the United Nations. He recently separated from his wife Jane Fonda, who then reintroduced herself to Hollywood as a presenter at the recent Academy Awards. She had promised to donate the gown she wore to the show to the Georgia Campaign for Adolescent Pregnancy Prevention so it could be auctioned off to raise funds. But "I've changed my mind," Fonda has announced. "I'm not auctioning it off after all. Seriously, I can't just wear this dress for 10 minutes on Oscar night and then turn it over to someone else yet." (AP) *...Some say Turner split from Fonda out of boredom. Nope: exasperation.*

Safe Insex: Researchers at New York's Cornell University say that by manipulating hormones, they may be able to develop a "safe and effective" method of birth control — for cockroaches. "They are the target of tons of neurotoxin pesticides every year but they keep coming back for more," says Cornell entomologist Jeffrey Scott. Limiting roaches' ability to reproduce could help get rid of them without using dangerous chemicals. However, Scott cautions, work on the method could take a while. "Don't expect roach birth control on your store shelves tomorrow." (Reuters) *...So in the meantime, we will still have to use the same old roach condoms.*

Unsafe Insects: A TV commercial for Orkin Pest Control is bugging viewers. During the ad a roach crawls across the screen, and some people don't realize it's part of the commercial. "Apparently, when you're sitting in your darkened den it seems pretty real," says a spokesman for the ad agency that created the spot. To heighten the effect, the ad usually runs at night. Orkin has announced a contest for people who admit the commercial "got me". The grand prize: a new TV set. They apparently got the idea from two viewers who damaged their TV sets by trying to kill the televised bug. "Both of them were very startled and they wanted us to fix their TVs, but that's not going to happen," said a spokeswoman. (AP) *...If "Wisk" couldn't be held liable for all the sui-*

cides over the "ring around the collar" campaign, Orkin sure isn't going to help people who smashed their own TV sets.

Gotcha II: A Canadian Internet company set up a gag web site on April Fool's Day promising free gas to anyone who filled out a "simple form." Skeptical surfers who checked out the registration for the site, purportedly put up by OPEC, indeed saw it was registered — falsely — to the "Organization of Petroleum Exporting Countries" in Austria. Those who fell for the hoax "were going to the gas stations and the gas operators were saying, 'We know nothing about this. What the hell are you talking about?'," admits a spokesman for JokeWeb.com, which pulled the stunt. But the joke may be on the jokers: the Toronto-based company has agreed to honor the free gas promise, offering one fill-up per month for the next six months to anyone who followed the directions on the fake web site. (Reuters) *...Next month, learn that "free gas" doesn't necessarily mean "free gasoline."*

What's in a Word? A poll by the Pew Research Center asked voters what words describe the top presidential candidates. George W. Bush was described with such "negative" words as "arrogant", "untrustworthy", "wimp" and "cocky", while the "negative" words used to describe Al Gore included "boring", "dull", "dishonest" and "incompetent". Another word frequently attributed to Gore was "politician", but that word was "undefined as to positive or negative." (AP) *...Certainly the voters know the answer to that.*

From Now On, it's "Barbie Woman": Lene Nystrom, the Norwegian singer best known for the song "Barbie Girl", says her recent breast implant surgery was not done to promote sales of her records, but rather to make her feel better about herself. "I've always been thin and flat-chested, in short very boyish. I just want to be more feminine," she said, rejecting criticism that she is setting a bad example for young girls. She also said she wants to get past being known for the "Barbie Girl" song. "I get the creeps when I'm compared with that doll. I have nothing in common with Barbie." (Reuters) *...Correction: she used to have nothing in common with Barbie.*

Equal Opportunity: Muslims in Gamle — "old town" Oslo, Norway — applied for the right to call worshipers to prayers, calling "Allahu akbar" ("God is great") over loudspeakers. The neighborhood council granted the request, to the delight of the World Islamic Mission. A spokesman said the decision is a "victory of great symbolic importance. It means our religion is respected on the same lines as other religions." But to keep things completely equal, the council also approved a request by The Norwegian Heathen Society to summon members to their meetings by calling out "There is no God" over the loudspeakers. (AP) ...*Next step: everyone screaming "Our God can beat your God" at the top of their lungs.*

Prior Restraint: Robert William Handley, 53, looks like Santa Claus. His car sports the plate "IMSANTA", and the Ohio man works holidays as a Santa. But Ohio Magistrate Thomas A. Stone has turned down Handley's legal petition to change his name to Santa Claus so that children won't be upset when he dies. "An obituary for Santa Claus would be the inevitable result of a name change to Santa Claus," Stone wrote in his decision. Handley says he will appeal. "Children who believe in Santa Claus generally don't read the paper," he said. And "they certainly don't read the obituaries." (AP) ...*Time magazine proclaiming "God is Dead": a quaint bit of history. A newspaper reporting "Santa Claus Dies": a catastrophe too burdensome to bear.*

And All of America Breathes a Huge Sigh of Relief

Strike Over, Twinkie
Shortage Ends
AP headline

In 'n' Out: A woman from Ft. Worth, Texas, stopped at her bank, did her business at the ATM outside, and left. Unknown to her, at the same time the bank was being robbed. As she drove away, a witness wrote down her license plate number and reported it as belonging to the robber's get-away car. As she pulled up to a friend's house, she was surrounded by police with their guns drawn. When the officers realized the 5-foot white woman didn't match the robber's description — a 5-foot-7-inch, 170-pound black man — they released her. "It was so humiliating," the unidentified woman said. "I thought maybe I'd run a stop sign or something when they started shouting for me to put my hands in the air." (Reuters) ...*No, for stop sign violations they start shooting right away.*

Catch Me If You Can: Ken Larsen, 34, was on the roof of a five-storey building in Walnut Creek, Calif., pulling cable. His co-worker yelled "Hold it a minute!", but it was too late: Larsen had stepped backward off the edge. On the way down, Larsen realized he was still holding the cable, so he grabbed it hard while his co-worker leaned on the spinning spool to slow his fall. Thanks to the cable — and some tree branches — slowing him down, he survived with just bruises and scratches. Amazed paramedics "told me to go buy a lottery ticket," Larsen said. "And I'm going to." (AP) ...*Better check him again: he may have brain damage if he thinks he can win California's lottery.*

Mananero Manana: With spring comes Daylight Savings Time. But Mexican Senator Felix Salgado doesn't like Daylight Savings one bit. "It affects good marital relations," he said in a Congressional debate. Many people "make love when they wake up, the so-called 'mananero' ("morning quickie"), but now when you wake up your partner is no longer there because she had to take the kids to school." (Reuters) ...*Either that, Felix, or she can't stand to see you in the light of day.*

The Beat Goes On: When Henry Nelson Jr., 20, and Jon Driggers, 26, pleaded guilty to creating "loud and offensive noise" by turning up the music in their cars, Rapides Parish, La., District Judge Tom Yeager wanted to come up with an appropriate punishment. He asked them what kind of music they liked in order to figure out what they don't like. He decided on Country Western, and sentenced them to attend a three-hour Country "music appreciation" session. "We're gonna crank that crap up while they're in there," Judge Yeager promised. "If they want all that bass, we're going to give it to them." And just in case they hate country as much as the judge, "I'm going to put them in a room without a window because I'm afraid they'd jump." (AP) ...*The real punishment comes later: deafness from their own loud music.*

Link Me: Christine Bergmann, Germany's Minister for Women and Families, likes reaching out to her constituents through her web site. And she likes to promote German businesses with a "Link of the Month". But the choice of Powercat for a link may have been ill advised. Although it offers cooking tips and links to local churches, it also offered the services of gigolos and pornography. After the Bild newspaper pointed out the link with the headline "Families Minister Offers Call-Boys!", the minister had the link section blocked, noting "This example demonstrates the dangers that arise from the technical possibilities of the Internet." (Reuters) ...*As usual, computers get the blame.*

Of the People: "I think being named Elvis Presley works in my favor, but it also works against me," says Elvis Aron Presley. The Elvis impersonator, who legally changed his name to that of his rock idol, is running for mayor of Phillips, Wis. "I doubt he stands a chance of winning, but stranger things have happened," says City Councilman Keith Corcilius. Presley, a tavern keeper, says he was inspired to get into politics by seeing the success of pro wrestler Jesse Ventura, now the governor of Minnesota. "If the people of that state can put a wrestler in office, I don't see what's wrong with the people in Wisconsin electing an Elvis impersonator," Presley says. (AP) ...*Politics: the New Vaudeville.*

By the People: Suspicious police officers in Lexington, N.C., pulled over Jose Guadalupe Pedro-Cruz, 33, after he picked up a package from the post office. They asked if they could search his car, and he said yes. They looked in the package, arrested Pedro-Cruz, and announced the department's "largest methamphetamine bust". Pedro-Cruz was charged with drug trafficking and held in jail for nearly two weeks while more tests were done. That's when they discovered the "flour-looking substance" they seized was flour, and the "waxy-looking blocks" were Mexican candy made from squash. Pedro-Cruz was released. Capt. Mike Brown said that field drug tests are "not 100 percent reliable," but added "we have done everything in good faith." (Lexington Dispatch) ...*Except maybe asking Pedro-Cruz what was in the package.*

For the People: A study by the Internal Revenue Service finds that members of Congress and their staffs are $10.5 million in arrears on their income taxes. As of the first of the fiscal year, 8.4 percent of the House of Representatives' employees were late on paying taxes, and 7.5 percent of the Senate's. The IRS didn't just single out Congress, however. They also noted that 8.2 percent of FBI employees are in arrears, as are 9.2 percent of Education Department employees and 8.1 percent of the general public. However, only 3.8 percent of the Treasury Department, which includes the IRS, are late. (AP) ...*You bet: they're the only feds who really know how nasty the IRS can be!*

Proof He's Just as Qualified as Dan Quayle
Gore Helps Kids Learn Gibberish
AP headline

Cocky: The town of Fruita, Colo., wanted something a little less boring than the usual "pioneers" to focus on for Colorado Heritage Week, so the city revived the story of Mike the Headless Chicken. In the 1940s, farmer Lloyd Olsen went to get a chicken for dinner. Wanting to leave as much of the neck as possible, he lopped off the chicken's head as tightly as he could. The chicken did not die, and continued to "peck" for food as it walked around the yard. Amazed, Olsen started feeding the chicken with an eye-dropper. The headless bird, dubbed Mike, appeared in *Life* magazine and traveled to exhibitions around the country. Fruita's Mike the Headless Chicken Festival is a smashing success, and a new Mike sculpture ("I made him proud-looking and cocky," the artist says) was recently unveiled downtown. Mike lived for 18 months after his head was chopped off. (AP) ...*Big deal: politicians can live like that for decades.* *

I See the Light! The British Tomato Growers' Association encouraged its members to try using *feng shui,* an ancient Chinese practice to create harmonious environments by channeling energy flows, to increase the yields of their gardens. That didn't sit well with two employees at Arreton Valley Nurseries on the Isle of Wight. "It put me in conflict with my faith," complains Martin Kelly, who quit the nursery and took his son Paul with him. "I'm not working for a farm that openly claims it relies on a power other than God." (Reuters) ...*You mean like the sun?* **

---

* See http://www.thisistrue.com/mike.html for photo

** See http://www.thisistrue.com/chi.html for the *major* fallout over this tagline

Chip Off the Old Block: When Gregory W. Kasey Jr., 20, of Maryland was accused of violating the terms of his probation, his 41-year-old father, also named Gregory W. Kasey Jr., took the rap and got a four-year prison term. It wasn't that big a deal, really: the elder Kasey was already serving 20 years for assault with intent to murder. When the judge discovered the mixup, he had the younger Kasey brought in and taken to jail. Asked what he thought of his father's action, he said "It showed me he still cares." Meanwhile, Gary Graham, 38, is awaiting execution after being convicted of murder during a 1981 robbery in Houston, Texas. His son, Gary Hawkins, 21, has just been charged with capital murder after a robbery-shooting in Houston. If Hawkins receives the death penalty, the two will become the only father-son pair on death row in Texas. "Obviously Gary Graham's been gone for a whole lot of time and hasn't had an influence" during the son's upbringing, a Houston police spokesman said. (AP) ...*No, it looks like he had a huge influence indeed.*

For Example: Selfish! Yes, says Britain's Princess Anne, Queen Elizabeth II's only daughter, Britons who live alone are plain inconsiderate of others. "Most people would call it independence, but I'm not that sure what that means. It could mean just plain selfish," the princess says. "It could be more convenient just to live all by yourself but it means that you don't understand the impact of your life on other people's lives," she says. "It's no good." (Reuters) ... *"Thus," she argued, "to be a good citizen you must follow my example and make your mummie hire dozens of servants to live with you."*

Mommie Dearest II: After Francisco "Paco" Tirado, 18, was convicted of killing two women during a gang initiation rite in Fayetteville, N.C., his mother came to court to testify as a character witness at his sentencing. But Alice Tirado was stopped outside the court by the deputy because she was drunk — tests showed her blood-alcohol level was 0.27 percent, more than three times the state's standard for intoxication. The judge sent her to jail to dry out. Her son faces either life in prison or the death penalty. (AP) ...*See? She should never have let him live alone.*

Step on It: Britain's Department of Environment, Transport and the Regions says London is getting rather congested with traffic. Their study shows that the average 3.9-mile trip between inner and central London now takes 40 minutes by car, as compared to 46 minutes by train, 62 minutes by bus, and 35 minutes by bicycle. The average 1.7-mile trip between two points in central London takes 29 minutes by car, 32 minutes by train, 40 minutes by bus, and 18 minutes by bicycle. (Reuters) ...*On the other hand, if you didn't have to go out in order to have company the traffic wouldn't be so bad.*

Slow Down: Philadelphia, Penn., police officer Margo Grady, a four-year veteran, was asked to transport a victim from a local hospital to the police department's Special Victims Unit. Grady got lost. Very lost. After driving more than 70 miles and crossing into New Jersey, Grady spotted another patrol car near the Newark airport, pulled it over with her lights and siren, and asked a surprised New Jersey state trooper for directions. He pointed her back toward Philadelphia, "and he wished me good luck," Grady wrote in a report to her superiors. The department had issued an all points bulletin and sent a helicopter to look for her, so she added "My apologies for any inconvenience or embarrassment to the police" to her report. (AP) ... *"For any"? Try "the extreme".*

Yes Dear: Michael Sgalla was having a fight with his girlfriend Pam DeVincent at his trailer home in Morgantown, W.Va. Sgalla grabbed a .38-caliber revolver, handed it to DeVincent and said if she hated him so much, she should shoot him. Sgalla says she did just that, hitting him in the shin. She has been charged with endangerment with a firearm. Sgalla was hospitalized. (Morgantown Dominion Post) ...*You always hurt the one you love. Just usually not quite so severely.*

How Do We Get These Two-footed Landies off Our Backs?

Dolphins, Whales, Seals
Do Research

AP headline

Peeeved: The landlords of an apartment complex in Radeburg, Germany, say men using the toilets in their apartments are splashing the radiators, which is causing them to rust. Thus, they say, from now on men must sit down while urinating. No way, say male residents. "I'm not going to let anybody tell me how I take care of business," says one. "I'm going to carry on standing." (Reuters) ... *The headline: "Men Say They Won't Stand for Sitting Down".*

Do it Yourself: Police in Albuquerque, N.M., say Edward Hall, 50, stole a utility trailer from a Home Depot store by hitching it to the back of his pickup truck and driving away. A few miles from the store, it came loose and crashed beside the road, so he went back to the store and stole a second one. The second also came loose and crashed just 75 yards from the first. As a Bernalillo County Sheriff's deputy investigated the crashes, Hall clipped the deputy's parked patrol car with, yes, a third trailer as he drove by. A chase ensued as Hall tried to get away — at a mere 25 mph, "probably because he knows the trailers, at high speeds, don't stay on very well," a detective said. Hall was charged with possession of burglary tools, three counts of unlawful taking a motor vehicle, and leaving the scene of an accident. (AP) ...*However, he's been signed to do a series of Home Depot commercials with their new slogan, "Take it From Us!"*

Home Improvement: Britain's Consumer Affairs Minister Kim Howells just launched a new safety campaign to reduce accidents during "do-it-yourself" projects, which are said to injure 250,000 Britons, 70 fatally, per year. Then he went home to build a rockery in his garden. "There was a piece of concrete sticking out as I was dismantling an old wall," he said. "I got a piece of wood to whack it free instead of fetching a suitable tool. Unfortunately I missed and smashed my finger." (Reuters) ...*Not having the suitable tool was probably lucky, since that could have really hurt him.*

Bang Bang, You're Dead: "This is a no tolerance policy. We're very firm on weapons and threats," announced district superintendent William L. Bauer. Armed teen-aged students threatening to blow up their school? No, several kindergartners at Wilson School in Sayreville, N.J., were playing "cops and robbers" on the playground, using their pointed fingers as "guns" and saying they were going to "shoot" each other. Principal Georgia Baumann suspended four students for three days under the district's zero tolerance weapons policy, and Bauer announced his support of the suspensions to the media. (AP) *...Could be worse: in the old days the kids' guns would have been confiscated.*

Aw, Shoot: Michael Hagood, 9, told a classmate at Upper Elementary School in Plainsboro, N.J., that he was going to "shoot" another classmate — with a wad of paper. By using the word "shoot", school officials say, Hagood triggered the school's zero tolerance weapons policy. But the time administrators found out, school was out for the day — so police officers were sent to his house after midnight, rousting the boy out of bed to question him. Once the cops realized the lack of a crime they left, but school officials required the boy go through a psychological examination and suspended him. His father is considering suing the school. (Trenton, NJ, Times) *...That's nothing: the principal is already preparing charges against the school photographer, who admits to "shooting hundreds of students" on school grounds.*

Poetic Injustice: An 11-year-old sixth-grader in Mamaroneck, N.Y., said something "rude" in the schoolyard. His parents had offered to make him apologize, but the school insisted on a five-day suspension for sexual harassment. That's when they hired a lawyer, who got the boy reinstated to school after three days. Attorney Ronald Kuby said the case was an example of "political correctness gone berserk," adding the boy "had never heard the term 'sexual harassment' and may not even know what sex is." What, exactly, did he do? He stepped up to two girls on the playground and chanted, "Roses are red / Violets are black / Your chest is as flat / As your back." (AP) *...Perhaps he knows what sex is after all.*

I'm Gonna Make You Eat That Gun: Clarion County, Pa., school bus driver Angelo Salvo panicked and screeched to a stop when he saw student Jamie Hinderliter, 16, "waving a gun around." He raced back to confiscate it as other students "doubled up in laughter." He found out why when he looked at the gun: it was made of chocolate. The boy's father agrees Jamie was "clowning around on the bus" and "should be punished without being fined," but Union High School officials are pressing criminal charges of disorderly conduct. And where did the boy get the gun-shaped candy? The school sold it to him as part of a fund-raising drive. (Pittsburgh Post-Gazette) *...If schools were subject to real-world law, that would be called entrapment.*

Bodycheck, Mate: Hockey, always. Baseball, often. Basketball, sometimes. But fights among players during chess matches? Never! Until Australia's Grand Prix chess tournament got into full swing, anyway. Players David Beaumont and Alexander Gaft came to blows after Gaft, who had finished his match in the fourth round of the prestigious Doeberl Cup in Canberra, allegedly disturbed Beaumont, who was still playing his match against another player. The Australian Chess Federation is considering banning both players. "Beaumont was sorely provoked but retaliation is no excuse," said chief arbiter Shaun Press. "How can an intellectual pursuit degrade itself in this way?" (Reuters) ...*They should have expected that the moment Fox won the TV rights.*

Head Over Heels: A 15-year-old girl playing the Easter Bunny at the West Towne Mall in Madison, Wisc., took off her bunny head during a break and put it down. Police are unclear what the problem was, but she and her assistant then began to argue. That's when "her assistant pushed her and she fell over her head," a police spokesman said. "The Easter Bunny then got up and punched her assistant a couple of times." The bunny and her 20-year-old assistant were both arrested. Meanwhile, security officers at the Janesville Mall in Janesville, Wisc., say they saw a man steal a pair of shoes and pursued him, but lost him in the crowd. When they reviewed a security tape of the incident, they recognized him as the man hired to play the mall's Easter Bunny. They allegedly found the shoes in his changing area and arrested him. "In my 27 years of doing this, nothing like this has ever happened before," said the mall manager, who added that Santa Claus had never been arrested at the mall. (AP, Milwaukee Journal Sentinel) ...*Battling beheaded bunny being busted was only the beginning; bemused bulls bust buffoon buddy bunny that bumbled when boosting booties.*

Leave John Elway Alone!

Old Guy Found Wandering at Stadium

AP headline

Waste Not, Want Not: Holyoke Hospital in Holyoke, Mass., is no longer discarding used scrub suits worn by doctors and nurses. Thanks in part to a scrub chic engendered by such hit TV shows as *Chicago Hope* and *E.R.*, it's selling them instead. Sure, they've been splattered with blood and other contaminants, "But that's the cool part! Don't you get it?" asks Kathy Buckley, the hospital's vice president of marketing. The scrubs are laundered, printed with a logo to set them apart from scrubs still in use at the hospital, and sold for $24.95 each piece, top or pants. Yes, Buckley admits, that's higher than new, but those have "never seen real action." (AP) *...And neither have the people buying the used ones.*

Friendly Fire: The Russian destroyer *Burnyi* was in port at Vladivostok when an "unsanctioned shot" was fired by one of its weapons. The shell hit the *Admiral Vinogradov*, an anti-submarine ship which was also in port, causing severe damage but no injuries. The incident occurred during a "planned check of weapons and machinery," a Pacific Fleet spokesman said. (Reuters) *...The classic "we were cleaning it and it went off" excuse.*

Kill 'em All and Let God Sort 'em Out: Religious broadcaster and former presidential aspirant the Rev. Pat Robertson and "Moral Majority" founder the Rev. Jerry Falwell finally disagree on something. Robertson says he believes the death penalty is morally justified, but thinks it's applied in a discriminatory manner and "doesn't provide enough opportunities for mercy." Falwell, on the other hand, thinks executions should be speeded up. "While courts do make mistakes," Falwell said, "I do not believe the mistake level is at the point where we need to rethink our whole system, and I personally believe that we need to reduce the time between conviction and execution." (AP) *...Thereby increasing the "mistake level" to a point where we need to rethink the whole system.*

Dumpster Diver: An audit of the Denver, Colo., police department's property room found that $100,000 in cash — mostly evidence from crimes — is missing. Chief Gerry Whitman says the money has probably been stolen and launched a criminal investigation. But Eric Russell, a 33-year-old former employee of Waste Management of Colorado, has come forward to say he thinks he knows where the money is: in the trash. Russell says he picked up trash from the dumpsters in the locked basement of the police station every day from 1994 to 1998, and "routinely" found money in the trash. "There were all kinds of things there," he says. "I found knives, evidence bags ... awful crime scene photographs, and objects tagged as evidence in cases. I once found a handgun, but that was broken." Some things he sold at flea markets, but threw away any drugs he found. The police are asking for the return of any items he still has, and say they have changed their disposal procedures. (Denver Rocky Mountain News)...*It's obvious he's right, considering he retired at age 31.*

The ABCs, Easy as 1-2-3: An argument has raged for years over the best way to teach reading: phonics, or whole language. After three years of study, a Congressional panel says the best way to teach reading is to stop fighting over which approach is better and use both. Andrew Hartman, director of the National Institute for Literacy, says the apparently lengthy report from the panel needs to be summarized for state lawmakers so they can introduce appropriate legislation. "Expecting people to read big, thick reports is unrealistic," he said. (AP) ...*Especially if they don't know how.*

What Aria Learning in School? Sentencing young offenders to listen to music they don't like seems to be catching on [*The Beat Goes On*, p120], so Eastern Connecticut State University in Willimantic decided to try the tactic with students who break campus rules. But the punishment doesn't seem to be working out the way administrators intended. "It was awesome," sophomore Kevin Bochiccio, 19, said about the production of *Tosca* he was sentenced to attend for having beer in his dorm. "I loved the show," agreed another student. "It's definitely not punishment. It's a privilege." At least one student in the audience was there voluntarily — he so enjoyed his sentence to watch *The Magic Flute* last semester that he now goes to the opera regularly. (AP) ...*You better shape up, young man, or it'll be season tickets for you!*

I Spy: His name is Bond. James Bond. Well, James Bond Nguyen, anyway, and he's been arrested in Vietnam and charged with fraud, not spying. Still, Ho Chi Minh City People's Court wanted to make sure Nguyen, who changed his name from Nguyen Van

Bon, isn't mistaken for anyone else. "He is not the 007 secret agent," a court official said, apparently with a straight face. (Reuters) ...*No, but we'd be happy to do a prisoner exchange and give you Pierce Brosnan.*

Short and Sweet: The night clerk at Kelly's Gas in Davenport, Iowa, said a man wearing a black ski mask came in just before midnight and pulled a gun from his pocket. "I want your money," the man said. The unnamed clerk looked at the robber and uttered two words: "Don't even." The surprised robber answered "O.K.," put the gun back in his pocket, and left empty-handed. (AP) ...*Wow: that works even better than "cellmate's wife".*

You Can't Touch This: City officials in Lafayette, Ind., are trying to figure out what to do about Kim Mattes. An exotic dancer, Mattes practices her routines in her front yard. For two years, neighbors have seethed, but now that she's installed a 10-foot pole in the yard, the display is really starting to get attention. "Law enforcement people indicate that she's just right on the fine line of crossing over into probably what's deemed public indecency," says Tippecanoe County Commissioner John Knochel. "She knows the law. When law enforcement officers have been out there before she's quoted it to them, so she's very aware of what she's doing." Officers can't help but notice her: her house is across the street from an Indiana State Police office. (AP) ...*They can't do anything to her, but they're going to do their best to touch her 10-foot pole.*

You Knew the Job was Dangerous When You Took It

British Soldiers Sue over Stress in Battle

Reuters headline

They've Flipped: The announced merger between Chevron Corp. and Phillips Petroleum Co. hit a minor snag when it came time to name the new, combined, company. "Lots of names were suggested," a Chevron spokesman said, but it came down to Chevron wanting Chevron-Phillips, and Phillips wanting Phillips-Chevron. To decide, the companies had a special gold coin struck, and a group of executives tossed the coin. Chevron-Phillips won. (AP) ...*Call it: heads the oil companies win, tails the gas-buying consumers lose.*

Decision Flopped: Murder, or manslaughter? A jury in Jefferson County Circuit Court in Louisville, Ky., couldn't quite decide, so they flipped a coin. Murder, came the verdict against Phillip Givens, 28, who was charged with killing his girlfriend. Rumors of the jurors' decision method buzzed around the courthouse and eventually got back to Judge Kenneth Conliffe, who declared a mistrial. "It's something I read about in law school," said Givens' lawyer, "but something I've never seen in 15 years of trial practice." (Reuters) ...*Yep, in Kentucky they usually cut a deck of cards.*

Honey, it's for You: Accident investigators say the car was airborne for about 150 feet before crashing through the roof of Joanne and Mahlon Donovan's house in Derry, N.H., at 3:00 a.m. Driven by a 20-year-old woman who was later arrested for drunk driving, the car came through the ceiling and dropped right over the Donovan's bed. "The thing was right in front of my face," Mr. Donovan, 65, said. "I could feel the heat from the exhaust system coming through the sheets." Still, that wasn't enough to wake his wife. He had to shake her awake after the crash. (AP) ...*There go any awards for "emotional damages".*

A 1001 Uses! Gemini Wink, 26, of Louisville, Ky., realized he was lost. While visiting a friend in Tampa, Fla., Wink waded into a swamp to shoot pictures of alligators. Taking along a roll of duct tape to mark his path, he was ready to head back around dusk when he couldn't find his marks. Afraid he would be eaten by 'gators when he fell asleep, he climbed 40 feet up a tree to keep out of their reach and — using his ever-more-handy roll — taped himself to a branch for the night. Wink's friend called for help when he didn't return by dark, and sheriff deputies found him in the tree, just 400 yards from his friend's house, so securely taped down that deputies had to climb up to help free him. (Reuters) ...*Next week, Wink will demonstrate his new duct tape tiger snare during a breathtaking adventure in India. Don't miss it!*

OK, Buddy, Cough Up the Evidence: After a jewelry store clerk said Rudolf Nyari, 64, of Hurst, Texas, had stolen a diamond tennis bracelet, police in Dublin, Ohio, searched him and his car.

They didn't find it. "At first he denied he had the bracelet," a police detective said. "But once we told him we had the X-ray, he chuckled and joked." Officers had obtained a search warrant — of Nyari's body. An X-ray showed he had swallowed the $17,000 bracelet, and it was still in his throat. "He drank several glasses of water and smoked cigarettes to build up enough phlegm to cough it up," the detective said. "It took about an hour." (AP) *...There you are, kids: the glamorous real life of a jewel thief.*

Sky-High Property Values: Plastic surgeon Dr. William Moore rented a backhoe to do some serious work in his yard in Boxford, Mass. It wasn't long before he called the gas company to report a "strong smell" of natural gas — he apparently ruptured a gas main with the heavy equipment. Three minutes later, he called the gas company again. "The house exploded as he was making the second call," said a gas company spokesman. "He said, 'Forget it. The house is gone.'" The five-bedroom home was worth about a half-million dollars. The spokesman said Dr. Moore did not call before he started his project to find out if there were any gas lines in the area he was digging. (Boston Herald) *...Huh: apparently it* ***does*** *take a brain surgeon to know to check that first.*

Where There's Smoke, There's Fire: A year-long study by England's University College London and the San Luis hospital in Palencia, Spain, finds that smoking reduces smokers' intelligence. "Our results indicate that persistent cigarette smoking into late life increases the risk of cognitive impairment," said Dr. Martin Prince of UCL, adding that the results are consistent with previous studies showing smoking reduces blood flow to the brain. (Reuters) *...Either that, or people who smoke are dumber to begin with.*

You're a Unique Individual, Just Like Everyone Else: Despite strong opposition from parents, the city of Philadelphia, Pa., became the first large city in the U.S. to adopt a uniform requirement for all public-school students. "We need to be dealing with kids who cannot read or write," complained a parent. "People who make suggestions like this are people who don't spend any time in school." But to no avail: the policy goes into effect immediately. School administrators seem to like the idea, however. "I think it will help add to uniformity of thought," argued middle school principal Bruce Ryan. Yes, agreed teacher Bayyinah

Abdul-Aleem, "I think it would really help because it would bring some sort of like-mindedness." (AP) ...*Isn't that why Nazi Germany adopted uniforms for school kids?*

Pandamonium: Zoo authorities in China are concerned over the dwindling population of pandas. "The real problem is that many pandas do not know how to mate," says Zhang Hemin, director of the China Giant Panda Research and Conservation Center in Sichuan. It doesn't help that 60–80 percent of the males are impotent, making it hard to impregnate females. He's considering giving pandas Viagra as a "last resort," but that may not be enough, he says. "As part of the pandas' education, we make those which are sexually inept watch videos of other pandas having sex." (AFP, Reuters) ...*Perhaps implausibly, pandering to persnickety impotent Pandas with pills and porn will possibly improve pregnancy percentages. Imprudent? Probably, unless public perceives progress.*

Clothes Make the Man: "I expect my deputies to be aggressive against criminals," growls Sheriff Everett Rice of Largo, Fla. "But I don't want them walking around looking like the Gestapo." Effective immediately, deputies may not wear black gloves anymore because people complained they made the lawmen look like "thugs". Officers buy their own gloves, a department spokesman said. (AP) ...*No problem: before long they'll all be changing to latex anyway.*

More Certified Experts Offer Their Tentative Conclusions

Shooting Suspect Said Hot-Tempered

—

Crashed Jet May Have Flown Too Low

AP headlines

Business is Hopping: Ray and Joey Strom of Arlington, Wash., say they have the ideal pet: kangaroos, wallabies, and wallaroos.

They're offering a four and one-half month baby wallaby for a startling $1,500. However, Ray points out, they're easier to care for than some other pets. "They don't dig, they don't make noise, they don't need vaccinations [and] their fur isn't supportive of fleas." (AP) *...But you do have to build a really high fence.*

Tastes Like Chicken: Chickens have long wandered around in downtown Sonoma, Calif., but something has riled them lately. The city council has approved a plan to round them all up and give them to area farmers after hearing reports that the chickens are "attacking" children who walk past them. "I don't know if it's possible to envision a rooster-less plaza," lamented Councilman Ken Brown. "But I have to tell you, when it comes to a question between a kid and a chicken, it's the kid." (Reuters) *...The fool probably decided that without even tasting a kid.*

Tastes Like Chicken II: University of Georgia engineering professor Takoi Hamrita has invented a small transmitter that is small enough to be implanted in chicks. A built-in processor will signal when they're too warm, since a major cause of chicken death is heat stress. She hopes eventually to monitor the birds' diets for optimum growth. "At the moment, the sensors tell us only the birds' deep-body temperature," Hamrita says. "Eventually, though, they will also tell us their respiration and heart rate." (AP) *...And in the final phase, it will signal the oven to turn off when roasting is complete.*

You Drive Me Crazy: "They've been fighting for 100 years like the Hatfields and McCoys," said Yonkers, N.Y., Police Commissioner Charles Cola. Finally, he said, Clunie Bernard, 40, "just snapped" after arguing with neighbor William Taino, 74. Bernard allegedly went home, got her car, and ran Taino over several times in his driveway. She has been charged with murder. Meanwhile, Sedonia Renee Martin, 22, was attending services at St. James Baptist Church in Covington, Ala., when she saw her husband, Tushaun Jamel Thompson, 24, look at another woman. After church, witnesses say, Martin tried to run Thompson down twice, but missed. "But her third try was the charm," a sheriff's spokesman said, with the impact "throwing him 20 feet into a ditch." He survived. Martin was arrested and charged with attempted murder. (AP, Reuters) *...Women are no less violent than men, they just choose different weapons.*

Germinated: The U.S. Army says a 33-year-old civilian microbiologist is partly to blame for his on-the-job illness. The unnamed scientist at Maryland's Fort Detrick was working on a vaccine for glanders, which more commonly infects horses but could be used in biological warfare. He came down with a fever, but did not report it for several weeks — until had developed liver and spleen abscesses and respiratory problems. By that time, he was severely ill with glanders and more difficult to treat. That's why early reporting is required by lab rules, a base spokesman said, but "I don't think anybody here is thinking about penalizing the employee right now." (AP) ...*Right: no sense in doing all that paperwork until you know he's going to survive.*

Can You Dig It? For the second time in a week [*Sky-High Property Values,* p132], a suburban Boston house has been leveled by a natural gas explosion caused by digging in the yard with heavy equipment. Off-duty Braintree, Mass., firefighter Joe Zanca was no fool: he hired a professional. Equipment operator Scott Volz was grading behind the house when suddenly there was a hissing sound. His boss came running but was thrown backward by the explosion moments later. "The house was fully engulfed in a ball of red," said Braintree Deputy Fire Chief Michael Carlino. No one was seriously injured, not even the Zancas' dog, which was inside the house. Fire officials noted the construction company did not check with the gas company before digging to find out where the gas line was. (Boston Globe) ...*Not only that, they've never stopped by the brain tree, either.*

Poetic Justice Dept: Stephanie Loudermilk, 29, has pleaded no contest to animal cruelty. The Okeechobee, Fla., woman and her husband Bryan made "crush" videos, in which Bryan filmed Stephanie stomping small animals such as rats and mice to death. In a plea bargain, Stephanie was sentenced to two years of probation, 300 hours of community service and psychiatric counseling. Bryan, however, was not in court: he died last year after accidentally being crushed to death under his own truck. (AP) ...*Of course, past customers wonder if she got that on tape.*

Next! Simon Beaufoy, who wrote the hit movie *The Full Monty*, is struggling to come up with an idea for a sequel. "It's a question I get asked once a week," he says — what will the plot be? But he can't come up with a workable story line. The original movie was about a group of unemployed men who turn to stripping to make money. Beaufoy's script earned him an Oscar nomination. "I've got to have an idea but I don't know what to do with these men," the Briton says. "They've taken their clothes off and I don't know what to do next." (PA) ...*Ask any woman: they'll tell you that's common in men.*

I Know You Are, But What Am I? Wisconsin state Rep. Jeff Plale is so sick and tired of rude politicians he's asking his colleagues to sign a pledge to be civil. "The time has come that we stop acting like Democrats and Republicans, and we start acting like legislators and we start acting like grownups," he says. The pledge urges legislators to "Treat your colleagues with respect and courtesy" and "Behave in a professional manner." Perhaps the concept should spread. Alabama state Rep. Skippy White took umbrage at Rep. Alvin Holmes' support for a resolution White opposed. Holmes declared "I'm not scared of nobody in here" and White confronted him. "You go to hell," Holmes told him. "You go there, too," White replied. "Go straight to hell," Holmes emphasized. That's when White threw a punch, which caused colleagues to step in and drag them apart. (AP, 2) ...*Big deal — pretty much all politicians go to hell anyway.*

Smoooooth! A fire at the Wild Turkey distillery in Lawrenceburg, Ky., destroyed 17,000 barrels of up to 15-year-old bourbon, causing a massive spill of flaming liquor into the Kentucky River. Officials say that is the cause of a massive fish kill in the river several days later, but the state Division of Water has assured the public the water is safe to drink. (AP) ...*Especially on the rocks with a twist.*

Woof
Listen Up, Your Dog Wants to Tell You Something
Reuters headline

A Menu as Long as Your Arm: Peter Johnson loves the All In One restaurant in Brighton, England. A lot. He not only eats there five days a week, he had the restaurant's name and phone number tattooed on his forehead. All In One's owner Nasser Bandar says he doesn't give Johnson free food, "because he did it on his own free will. But whenever he comes in, he'll go straight to the front of the queue." Johnson, 49, says the tattoo is no big deal. "Some people, including my family, think I am crazy. But I like tattoos, so why not?" (AP) ...*Because someday they might change their phone number.*

First Class: The U.S. used B-2 bombers during the Kosovo conflict, flying them out of U.S. bases. The resulting 30-hour missions might normally have been taxing for the two pilots, but they were able to take turns sleeping during the long flights. Unfortunately, the billion-dollar planes have no place for pilots to sleep. No problem: the Air Force fitted "lounging lawn chairs" into the cockpits. The chairs were purchased at Wal-Mart for $8.88 each. (Reuters) ...*Naturally, the wing commander has been severely disciplined for not coming up with a multi-million-dollar solution.*

Not Accountable: An audit by the General Accounting Office finds that the U.S. Department of Defense's books are off. Way off. The Pentagon does not need $36.9 billion worth of the items it has in its possession, and about a trillion dollars worth of inventory is not properly tracked. The Pentagon says it will be several more years before it updates its systems enough to know what all that it owns, and where it is. (AP) ...*Why is the drug trade a threat to "national security", but billions of dollars of missing weapons isn't?*

Read it Again and Again: When the Tennessee-based Cracker Barrel restaurant chain ran a promotion to give free books to libraries, customers thought it was a great idea. The libraries are a little less enthusiastic. The Gilbert, Ariz., library, for instance, isn't sure what to do with the 11,796 copies of a preschool book, 1,000 copies of *Quick and Easy Pasta* and 200 copies of *How To Use Microsoft Windows 95* it received. "We can find a creative way of doing something with the children's books," said county library director Harry Courtright, "but Windows 95 is of no value to anybody." The restaurant chain said it did not get a chance to review the titles. It didn't say what it would do to make up for the useless gifts. (Arizona Republic) ...*Maybe the library can send them a few hundred copies of* In Search of Excellence.

Man of Steel: The town of Metropolis, Ill., is having a hard time finding a man to play Superman at their upcoming Superman Festival. The successful applicant must be tall, handsome, muscular, dark-haired, willing to strut around downtown wearing blue tights and, please, not have a southern drawl. But so far only balding men with pot bellies have applied. "I think these guys must have forgotten what Superman looks like," complains Jim Hambrick, owner of the town's Super Museum and co-chairman of the search committee. (AP) ...*At least they're ready when it's time to cast Lex Luthor.*

You've Got Male! According to Islamic law, a man can divorce his wife simply by telling her "I divorce you." A court in Dubai, United Arab Emirates, has been asked to rule on the legality of the divorce of a man who sent an e-mail to his wife with that message. (Reuters) ...*That's OK with her, since all he wanted was cybersex.*

It's an Ad Ad Ad Ad World: Race cars have them. Buses and taxis, too. Advertisements, that is. Why not your car, asks the California-based Autowraps, Inc. The company pays up to $400 per month to ordinary people willing to plaster their cars with ads. They already have about 200 drivers signed up. "A lot of people look when I'm driving," says a San Francisco woman with an ad-bannered car. "I vainly thought they were looking at me, and then I realized, no, they're looking at the car." (AP) ...*Get used to it: you're in California.*

God Save the Queen: "They are anarchists and they want the royal family dismantled," warns London's police chief, Sir John Stevens. "I think one of the royal family could be at risk." Yes, admits the group Movement Against the Monarchy, they're going to target the queen — for a mass public "mooning" outside Buckingham Palace. "We want 2,000 bare butts" pointed at the queen, a MAM spokesman said, adding that it would be a "cheeky" way to get publicity. (Reuters) ...*Perhaps, but the public may just think you're cracked.*

Hard Time: The Blantyre House prison on the Isle of Sheppey, Kent, England, is considered a "model" prison for its low rate of inmate drug abuse, low assault rate, and its progressive programs such as work release. But acting on tips, a police raid found escape equipment, forged drivers licenses, stolen credit cards, drugs, and large quantities of cash. The warden has been fired.

Meanwhile, inmates at the maximum security Caseros peniten-
tiary in Buenos Aires, Argentina, were running a car stripping
operation, officials found. Stolen cars were brought into prison
grounds, stripped, and sold as parts. (PA, Reuters) ...*Of course,
they didn't recycle the license plates, since that could put a friend
out of a job.*

After Every Election
Creepy, Crawly Creatures Invade DC
AP headline

Sticky Solution: The latest unproven health fad is using magnets to
relieve pain. No one has shown they work any better than a pla-
cebo, but Dr. Thomas Mattioni of the Arizona Heart Institute in
Phoenix has done a study that shows magnets indeed have a real
effect on some patients. The magnetic field can kill people who
have pacemakers or implanted defibrillators, so magnets should
be kept at least six inches from such devices, he says. For
instance, someone with a pacemaker and a magnetic mattress pad
could find their pacemaker shut off if they roll over onto their
stomach. (AP) ...*Worse, patients with metal plates in their heads
can get stuck in bed for days.*

I Vant to Be Alone: Edward Furtak, 43, said he was turning into a
chain-smoker and wanted to quit. So the Australian man went on
a walkabout in the outback — for six months. He told his wife and
mother he would return when he was ready, but they got worried
after they hadn't heard from him for three months. "I did make it
clear to everybody I would not be ringing," an irritated Furtak
said when he was found by police after his family reported him
missing. However, he said, the trip did cure him of smoking.
(Reuters) ...*So would a three-month internship at a cancer ward.*

Fall Dead, I Got You! As a cost-cutting measure, recruits at the
British Royal Navy's *HMS Cambridge* training facility near
Plymouth, are not given live rounds to shoot. Instead, trainees are
being taught to load dummy shells, set their aim, and yell "Bang!"
Sailors are calling the scheme a "joke", but a Navy spokesman

said live firing was no longer necessary, and that real shells cost more than the "value" received from firing them. On the other hand, the *Cambridge* isn't really a boat, either: it's a boat-like structure built on dry land next to the sea, with its guns mounted on concrete pads. (PA) ...*Which is just as well, since the recruits can't swim.* [*This is True: Cost of Being Poor Rising,* p43]

Sightseeing: A travel guide printed by Spain's government tourism office wants potential visitors to really get the feel of the place. "With mountains the same thing happens as does with women, that the desire they provoke is inversely proportional to the number of times you've got on top of them," the guidebook says. One mountain is described as "black, svelte...hard and slippy, like Naomi Campbell's loins." After Spanish citizens expressed their outrage over the descriptions, the government claimed the book had been "printed by mistake" and recalled all copies. (Reuters) ...*Now there's a writer who would be inspired by Wyoming's Grand Tetons.*

Childhood's End: New English textbooks in India will do away with many old nursery rhymes because they are too negative. "'Rain, rain go away' is a disastrous proposition in the Indian context," says Prof. Ramesh Dhongde of Pune, India. "So we changed this" to "Rain, rain come again." Dhongde says "we don't want children to feel threatened by a new language." Meanwhile, Britain's Education Minister Margaret Hodge has released a new booklet that urges a ban on the game musical chairs. "A little bit of competition is fine, but with musical chairs the competition is not fair because it is always the biggest and strongest children who win," said the book's author, Sue Finch. "Musical statues is better because everybody wins." (AP, Reuters) ...*Just like in real life.*

Childhood Already Ended: Headteacher Kevin Jones confirms that a student at Hall Cross School in Doncaster, England, hired a stripper to perform for classmates. About 150 pupils shouted encouragement as the performer, who charged the unidentified student 35 pounds (US$55), stripped down in the common room to nothing but "a pair of skimpy knickers." The performance was stopped when a teacher came into the room "and frogmarched the brunette out of the school gates." The student has been suspended. (PA) ...*The suspension lasts but days. The notoriety will last a lifetime.*

Who's Calling? The Utah state prison system has decided to end its prisoner phone soliciting program where inmates were hired as telemarketers. They were often given personal information by the people they talked to, but the prisoners were not required to identify themselves. Personal information was sometimes shared with other prisoners, including sex offenders, and at least one prisoner has been caught sending "flirtatious letters" to teen-aged girls. The inmates made calls for businesses such as SandStar Family Entertainment, and answered phones for some state agencies, including the Utah Department of Commerce and the Utah Travel Council. The program was similar to those in place in other states. (AP) ...*So before you yell at a telemarketer and slam down the phone, remember he knows your address and may soon be out on parole.*

I Protest: A candidate for mayor in Mexico City says that protests cause too many traffic jams in town, so there should be a special place for protesters to march and complain. "We need some kind of protestdrome or marchdrome," argues Tere Vale. "There would be an agreement with the media that would allow them to cover events without the rest of the citizens being affected." Several other candidates quickly expressed their support for the idea. (Reuters) ...*Especially when they saw that construction plans call for the entire floor to be a trap door.*

Dust to Dust

You Want To Be Buried on the Moon?

AP headline

Why the British Empire Isn't One Anymore — One In a Series: Jason Pitt and Bill Wood of Walsall, England, wanted to hire some new staff for their business. They called the local government-run jobs center to place an ad, but the center wouldn't allow its wording: they wanted to advertise for "hardworking and enthusiastic" employees. "They told us 'You can't put that, it's discrimination'," Wood said. A Walsall Jobcentre manager spokesman said the ad violated the Disability and Discrimination Act. Secretary of State David Blunkett personally intervened and ordered the agency to back down. (PA) ...*Now for the quiz. Which is more discriminatory? 1) Asking for a hardworking and enthusiastic employee. 2) Declaring that a disabled person can't be hardworking and enthusiastic.*

Godspeed: A convoy of seven Catholic bishops in Umbria, Italy, was pulled over by police. All seven drivers were cited for speeding at 135 kph in a 90 kph zone (86 mph in an 56 mph zone). One of the bishops explained they were trying not to be late to a speech by a cardinal. (Reuters) ...*And if "God is your copilot", He gets a ticket too.*

Motoring Madness II: Lorain, Ohio, police officer Joseph Kopronica pulled over a van because it appeared "out of control." He said the driver, Nancy M. Lang, 42, appeared drunk. But if he hadn't noticed that, Lang may have given him a clue: "Please give me a break," she asked him. "I'm drunk." After Lang failed a field sobriety test, he told her she was under arrest. She protested "Wait: I can do this!" and proceeded to do jumping jacks and a push-up. When she started to do a cartwheel, Kopronica stopped her "for her safety and mine." Lang has been charged with speeding, driving under the influence of alcohol, driving with a suspended license, and driving with expired license plates. (AP) ...*Any calisthenics can and will be used against you in a court of law.*

You Can Run, But You Cannot Hide: An unnamed psychologist in Freiburg, Germany, has been fined 2,400 marks (US$1,100) after jogging nude in a city park. The 50-year-old man had argued in court that "running around without clothes on is the most natural thing in the world" and that he had "even informed the police" before his runs. The court rejected his argument and ordered him to stop running naked in public. (Reuters) ...*If he thinks it's so "natural" why did he think it was necessary to inform the police?*

Of Course, You Could Always Just Rename the Town: The joke in Big Lake, Texas, is that there is no lake. Well, once in a while there is: the 1,000-acre lake is dry, and has only had water when someone has bothered to pump some in. And mayor J.R. Dunn wants to do just that, drilling 50–100 wells to feed the lake continuously. The project would cost at least $2 million, far beyond what the town of 3,500 people can afford. A spokesman for State Sen. Troy Fraser is dubious, noting the drought gripping the state. "The state's priorities have to be on drinking water and irrigation before recreational use," he said. Indeed, says a local resident, "The evaporation out here is so bad, you are looking at least a million gallons a day." But Mayor Dunn is undeterred. "We are sitting here living in a town called Big Lake and we don't have a lake," he whined. (AP) ...*Just paint the dirt blue and be done with it.*

Nonsense Nomenclature II: The town of Halfway, Ore., population 160, hasn't changed much since it renamed itself Half.com to become "America's first Dot-com city." The publicity stunt, dreamed up by the company that owns the Internet domain name, hasn't brought hoped-for tourists. "As far as boosting business in our town, I don't think it's done anything," said the owner of the only breakfast joint in town. Jerry Weir, the town's web master and deputy sheriff, agrees. "It's gotten the town a lot of publicity. Has it made the town a lot of money? No," he says. "Don't expect the Web to be your savior." (AP) ...*Especially when you have a half-assed business plan.*

Write Your Congressman: Sune Haggmark and Ann-Mari Remahn say tourists like their special home-made elk dung paper. Each sheaf of paper contains eight to 10 "elk pats" held together by "a secret binding agent," and costs 70 crowns (US$8). The Ostersund, Sweden, couple says the paper is "a light brown color shot through with traces of bark and small splinters." (Reuters) ...*Paper, fine. But who wants to lick the envelopes?*

Up On the Roof: "It wouldn't be a good life without a challenge," says Dave Anthony, who says he is "39, going on 15." A friend was tearing down his house in Kent, Washington, so Anthony came over in his 4×4 GMC pickup to help. First, Anthony knocked down the garage — by ramming it with his truck. He was helped along by an 18-pack of beer which, he said, he was drinking "before, during and after" what happened next: "I just got a wild hair," he said, and decided to drive his truck onto the roof. But the already partly-collapsed structure couldn't handle it, and started to buckle. A local towing company brought the truck down safely, but Anthony stopped laughing when they handed him a bill for $695 and, when he couldn't pay it, hauled his truck off to an impound yard. (Seattle Post-Intelligencer) ...*He may have stopped laughing then, but that's when everyone else started.*

Road Show

Man Executed in Texas, Oklahoma

AP headline

Be Prepared: John T. Levendosky, 52, "admitted to having always been fascinated with bondage and servitude and stated that he just wanted to see how people react in these situations," says the Pennsylvania State Police. Police say Levendosky, an assistant scoutmaster, took three Boy Scouts, aged 11, 12 and 13, on a camping trip, tied them up with rope, and "made them play several sadomasochistic games," but did not sexually assault them. He has been charged with endangering the welfare of children, corruption of minors, unlawful restraint, reckless endangerment, assault and harassment. (AP) ...*Pretty much no one on the jury is going to believe his claim that he doesn't know how to tie knots.*

Charity Begins at Home: Bob Sutton, 49, and his wife Jan founded the Bartimaeus Romania charity shop to raise money to build an orphanage for Romania's "sewer children". Sutton, a grandfather from Thornton Cleveleys, England, recently went to Romania and shortly announced plans to marry a 15-year-old girl from Timisoara — as soon as he can get divorced and the girl turns 16. "I have committed no other crime than to have fallen in love with a young girl," he insists. "She loves me back." However, he stresses, "I am not a pervert. Girls grow up faster in Romania and a 15-year-old girl here is different." (PA) ...*Isn't that pretty much what the perverts say?*

What Did You Learn at School Today? Aaron Lawton, 11, said he thought his teacher was just kidding when he told him, "If you miss an assignment, the whole class gets to deck you." But a month later, when the Franklin Township, N.J., sixth-grader was late on a homework assignment, math teacher Maxie Rivers allegedly lined up the students and had them take turns hitting him. "Some of the punches were hard, some were soft and some were in between," the boy said. Rivers' attorney said the beating was "light-hearted" and that the kids only "tapped him kiddingly," but a doctor found multiple bruises. Hillcrest School officials suspended the teacher with pay while they investigate the incident. (AP) ...*Somehow it seems fitting that "The School of Hard Knocks" is in New Jersey.*

First Aid: A study of injuries sustained by passengers of Britain's rail network found that 10 percent of the reported injuries involved the same person. The unnamed traveler reported a shoulder injury 49 times in a one-year period. "The injuries were reported at stations throughout the rail network, from Penzance to Edinburgh, sometimes twice in one day," a Railtrack spokesman said. However, the passenger apparently was not trying to perpetrate fraud: he never asked for compensation. (Reuters) ...*If someone would just get around to saying "sorry" he'll go away happy.*

Roger, Roger. What's the Vector, Victor? Flight controllers at Oakland International Airport in Waterford Township, Mich., speaking with an incoming corporate jet over the radio, clearly heard it in the background: "hijack". The pilot hadn't reported trouble, but perhaps a gunman was controlling what he could say. The tower called the police, which called in a squad of officers, the county SWAT team, and the FBI. But when the plane arrived, they discovered that someone had stepped into the cockpit to say hi to the co-pilot. His name is Jack. (AP) ...*When in doubt, ask.*

Beaver News: Sam Pshyshlak says a crazed beaver attacked her dogs — two 200-lb. Newfoundlands. "It pinned them. I never thought beavers were capable of that," said the Manitoba, Canada, farmer. "I've lost all respect for beavers. I never would have imagined this from a beaver." Meanwhile, Beaver College of Glenside, Penn., has decided to change its name. Beaver president Bette E. Landman says the name "too often elicits ridicule in the form of derogatory remarks pertaining to the rodent, the TV show *Leave It to Beaver* and the vulgar reference to the female anatomy." A committee has been formed to recommend a new name. "Beaver College doesn't really represent who we are anymore," said spokesman Bill Avington. (Reuters, AP) ...*Which is* *precisely the problem the frat boys have been complaining about.**

Non Compos Criminalis: A small post office inside a news stand in West Midlands, England, was robbed. Sort of. A woman brandishing a crowbar threatened the clerk, but the clerk refused to cooperate. In the ensuing struggle, the robber accidentally hit herself on the head with the crowbar, then cut herself with the hook end. Next, her shirt got caught on something and was torn off. That was enough: she fled with a male accomplice. A police spokesman hoped a witness would help break the case, noting "there must be someone out there who is aware of a couple ... running away from the premises, the female bloodstained with just her bra on at the time." The news stand owner was not particularly upset by the raid, noting "the post office was never in any danger. It was closed." (PA) ...*Sounds like she's a few diamonds short of a tiara.*

Next Case: The Mount Vernon Apartments near Fort Belvoir, Va., wanted to evict a disabled couple who was behind on their rent due to a reduction in their disability benefits. Deborah Morris and Louis Swann were behind $250, testified the apartment complex's lawyer, Andrew Lawrence, in court. "Consider it paid," said Judge Donald McDonough to the astonished attorney, and handed him the money out of his own pocket. Four other attorneys in the courtroom for other cases also offered to help the couple. And the apartment complex? Lawrence complained that the judge "embarrassed" his client. (Reuters) ...*No sir, the client quite competently embarrassed himself.*

A Spoonful of Sugar Helps the Medicine Go Down: A study led by the Veterans Affairs Medical Center in Honolulu, Hawaii, finds that coffee may help prevent Parkinson's disease — and the more coffee consumed, the better. "Hopefully, this will lead to more basic research on caffeine and its effect on areas of the brain affected by Parkinson's disease," said study leader Dr. G. Webster Ross. (AP) ...*Either way, you're gonna shake.*

Awwwwww: The U.S. Federal Trade Commission has ruled that any company that issues credit, such as banks and insurance companies, must keep customer names, addresses, and social security

---

* See http://www.thisistrue.com/arcadia.html for story update

numbers private unless customers allow them to share it. In the past, the so-called "credit header" information has routinely been shared for marketing, and for private investigators and collection agencies to track people down. The Direct Marketing Association is livid. "The breadth of [the new rule] goes to the extremes," sputters DMA president H. Robert Wientzen. "If we chip away at the availability of information about consumers, we're in danger of reducing some of the benefits consumers have gotten used to receiving." (Washington Post) ...*That's a risk we're willing to take.*

That's Often the Way it Works

Indicted Man Might Be Part of Plot

AP headline

Fame is Fleeting: Two girls, aged 16 and 17, were arrested in the murder of a friend, a 16-year-old girl, in San Fernando de Cadiz, Spain. The two girls allegedly told police the murder made them "feel good." Their motive? They said the killing would make them "become famous." Police refused to release the killers' names. (AP) ...*Good.*

Relapse: Employees at Northern General Hospital in Sheffield, England, have been put on alert to watch for a 29-year-old woman who keeps coming to the hospital and pretends to be a patient, a care-giver or a kitchen worker, and has been shooed away as many as seven times a day. "She has caused difficulties for our security and medical staff but all hospitals by the nature of the care they provide have to be open to the public," a hospital spokesman says. On at least one occasion, she showed up in the emergency department wearing "medical clothes", but she was "quickly spotted" and escorted out. (PA) ...*She sounds sick. She should be in a hospital.*

Re-Relapse: Gary Lee Stearley, 26, apologized for being late for the overnight shift at Mercy Hospital in Pittsburgh, Pa., and went to work. It wasn't until after the shift was over that he told his supervisors in the emergency room that he was not really a physician's assistant, and told police that he had a history of mental problems and was HIV-positive. "Do I think he had any malicious intentions? No," a police investigator said. "It more seemed he was acting out his passion to be an ER person." Stearley was arrested and charged with trespassing and false impersonation. Hospital workers said they were suspicious, but allowed him to work the shift because he "spoke medical jargon." (AP) ... *Great: all it takes to be qualified for ER duty is careful attention to* Chicago Hope *reruns.*

Prove It: So many live pensioners have been declared dead in Colombia that misclassified breathing people can apply at government offices for an official "Survival Certificate". Arturo Suspe, 87, was one such victim. His $133-per-month pension was canceled, so he went to Bogota to stand in line for his certificate. But before he could get to the front of the line, he dropped dead of a heart attack. (Reuters) ... *At least he was able to avoid a lot of red tape and paperwork.*

Love Thy Neighbor: An unidentified woman from Covington, Ga., came home from vacation to find her apartment looted. Not only furniture, but clothing, food from the cupboard and freezer, appliances, and cleaning supplies were gone. Police arrested her neighbor, Lakisha Weaver, and two of Weaver's friends for burglary, noting they treated the woman's apartment as their "own personal Wal-Mart." Meanwhile, two teenagers told police in Fort White, Fla., that their mother "made them" steal dishes, pots, pans, a TV and a bed — with its spare sheets — from a neighbor's house. Linda Diane Faulkner, 35, was charged with burglary, grand theft and contributing to the delinquency of a child. Her children were not arrested. (AP, 2) ... *Definitely not: they're the first kids in history to do what they were told.*

Picture This: Bill Easterbrook and his wife, Joan, were looking through a travel brochure when Joan turned the page and spotted a photo of her husband dancing with another woman at a swanky hotel. The woman was a "complete stranger," he insisted, and he swore he had never been to the hotel. Easterbrook thinks the photo was taken years ago when he was on a cruise — with his wife — and that the other woman had been spliced in with a computer. The travel company promises to delete it from their next brochure. Meanwhile, Leslie Brown of Clackamas, Ore., is suing

Vagrant Records for using her "embarrassing" high school prom photo on the cover of *Before You Were Punk 2*. Brown says she doesn't want to be reminded of her 80s hairstyle or her prom date. The suit asks for $100,000 and demands the photo be removed from the CD and Internet site promoting the record. Her prom date Jon Halperin gave the photo to the company and insists "it was just for fun. I didn't get paid for it." (PA, AP) *...Just like you didn't get anything on prom night, punk.*

The Writing is On the Wall: It's tough to find employees in a tight labor market, so the Swedish furniture maker Ikea is trying a new approach: attracting applicants with handwritten ads on the walls of public bathrooms. "After only four days we had received 60 applications. That's four or five times more than what we would get from a normal newspaper ad," said spokesman Jimmy Ostholm, adding that the unusual campaign was significantly cheaper than a newspaper ad, too. "In the toilet people are more relaxed and receptive to our message." (Reuters) *...That may work for applicants, but everyone else gets the message, "Ikea furniture is crap."*

Fixer Upper: Tracy Mayberry of Nashville, Tenn., complained repeatedly about the condition of her apartment, but nothing was done. In fact, she says, the manager threatened to evict her family. That's when she started calling the building's owner names, so the owner called her. "He said he'd heard I'd called him a slumlord, and I said I did," Mayberry confirmed. The building's owner, Vice President Al Gore, got an earful. "I said if you want to run for president, you ought to behave like a landlord should. He agreed with me. He said he's going to come in and do a complete renovation," she says. Gore's spokesman says the family will have to move while repairs are made, because so many are needed. But "I should emphasize for the record they're not being evicted." (AP) *...Though come November, Gore may be.*

Think So?

Gas Prices May Hurt
Winnebago Sales

AP headline

Extra Headlines . . . .

And Vice Versa

Weight Loss Helps
With Daily Chores
AP

• • •

Details, Details

You Can't Vote — You're Dead!
Reuters

• • •

Fizzy

Incoming Coke CEO
Continues Shakeup
AP

• • •

Especially when you use your Apple

Log-on a Day To
Keep Doctor Away
AP

• • •

Science Finally Tackles the Big Problems

Psychology of Bad
Hair Days Studied
AP

Work Now Begins on Figuring Out How to Divide It

Two To Share Mathematics Prize

AP

• • •

That'll Teach Him

UK Serial Killer Doctor Stripped of Salary

Reuters

• • •

Don't We All?

Companies Want To Reduce Cow Flatulence

AP

• • •

Erie is Missing

Panel Warns of Great Lakes Shortage

AP

• • •

Who Am I to Say it's a Typo?

N.Y. Yankees Shit Out Minnesota Twins, 2-0

Reuters

That'd be the Shits

Fecal Explosion Threatens City

Reuters

• • •

Sorry, No Room Left for the Story

Food: Dog Days Of Summer — Hard Times Hit The Hot Dog As Recalls Rise; Is That A Worm In My Wiener?

Wall Street Journal

• • •

Not Included in Port Fees

Cruise Line Discloses Sex Charges

AP

• • •

Not a Laughing Matter

Mormon Humor? Get Serious

AP

• • •

Hitting Below the Belt OK

Transvestite Boxer to Show Argentina Swing or Two

Reuters

Did You Pack Your Own Bag?
Has it Been Constantly Under Your Control?

Britain Arrests Man Over Body in Suitcase

Reuters

• • •

Ego-Driven Liar?

Clinton Compares Gore to Nixon

AP

• • •

But With Good Behavior, He Could Get Out
in Just 875 Years

UK "Human mole" to be Buried Alive for Millennium

Reuters

• • •

Charge It

Want to go bankrupt? That'll be $400 please

Reuters

• • •

South Park, The Movie

Canada Gears Up for Culture Battle with U.S.

Reuters

In the Car, or In the Driver's Seat?

Loose Screw Caused
Crash, Ferrari Says
Reuters

• • •

What Happens when Newspaper Guys Get
Their News from TV

Help! My Brain is Shrinking!
UPI

• • •

Just When You Think You Have Things Figured Out

Killer Suspected in
Unsolved Cases
AP

• • •

Call in the Picnics

Ant Colony on Verge
of Extinction
AP

• • •

Fighting Dirty

Politicians Fight Back With Laws
AP

"If They Hadn't Used Any, We'd Have Plenty"

British Water Firm Blames Customers for Shortage

Reuters

• • •

Petty Theft

Frankel May Have Stolen Only $50M

AP

• • •

Too Bad for the People Who Died Yesterday

Life Expectance Climbs 30 Years

AP

• • •

The Dead Heal So Slowly

Wounds Remain 10 Years After Killing

AP

• • •

Latest Medical Research Reveals

Dehydration Poses Threat to Survival

AP

Just Two Years Later
Molasses Spill Hits
Michigan River
AP

• • •

We're Sure It's Around Here Somewhere
Stealth Fighter Compromise
Elusive
AP

• • •

Why Didn't Anyone Think of This Before?
Oregon City Bans
After-School Fights
AP

• • •

Touchy
Public Shaming Bothers Woman
AP

And Last...

Another Grant, Another Study Result
Good Health Habits
Can Extend Life
AP

About the Author · · · · · · · · · · · · · · · · · · ·

Randy Cassingham has a university degree in journalism, but he could never quite deal with the concept of intruding on people in disasters to ask, "How do you *feel* about this?" Nor could he ever keep a straight face when presented with the outrageously silly situations that people tend to get themselves into that might make it into the "news". So, not counting brief stints as a writer and photographer on his school paper ("It doesn't count, it was a long time ago"), he has never been a reporter. Instead, he drove an ambulance in northern California (keeping a straight face *most* of the time), and since has been a search and rescue sheriff's deputy, commercial photographer, writer, editor, publisher, software engineer, consultant, curmudgeon and staff jester for various projects and companies. Randy and his wife (and the tom, Clancy, who really does love to sit and sleep on the back of Randy's chair) live in Boulder, Colorado.

There's Lots More *True* Where This Came From

This is True® compilations come out annually, pulling together a year's worth of columns plus *extra* stories and headlines that didn't fit into Randy's weekly newspaper space. Order the books through your favorite bookstore, or get them directly from us. Just be sure to "Get One for Every Bathroom in the House!"

The fastest way to order is online: see http://www.thisistrue.com

☐ Volume 1: *This is True: Deputy Kills Man With Hammer*

☐ Volume 2: *This is True: Glow-in-Dark Plants Could Help Farmers*

☐ Volume 3: *This is True: Pit Bulls Love You, Really*

☐ Volume 4: *This is True: Artificial Intelligence Like Real Thing*

☐ Volume 5: *This is True: Cost of Being Poor Rising*

☐ This Volume: *This is True: Platform Shoes Claim Another Life*

Each book is $11 plus shipping (see web site for shipping info)

☐ Check or Money Order enclosed

☐ Charge my: ☐ Visa   ☐ Mastercard   ☐ Discover   ☐ AmEx

    Card #_____-_____-_____-_____ (Exp: ___/___)

Name: _____

Address: _____

City _____ State/Prov: _____

Zip/Postal Code: _____ Country: _____

E-mail address: _____

Mail this form with payment to Freelance Communications, PO Box 17326, Boulder CO 80308 USA or see our web site for instant online ordering: http://www.thisistrue.com